afternoon tea parties

afternoon tea parties

SUSANNAH BLAKE
photography by Martin Brigdale

RYLAND
PETERS
& SMALL

LONDON NEW YORK

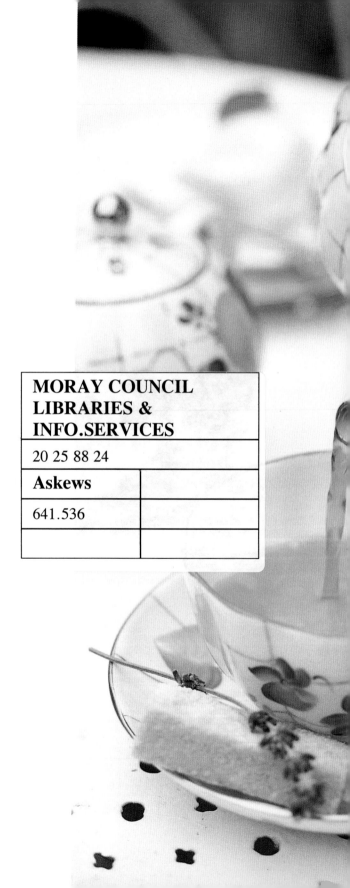

For the girls!

Designers **Pamela Daniels**
& Megan Smith
Senior editor **Julia Charles**
Production **Hazel Kirkman**
Art director **Leslie Harrington**
Publishing director **Alison Starling**

Prop stylist **Helen Trent**
Food stylists **Bridget Sargeson**
& Linda Tubby
Assistant food stylist **Stella Sargeson**
Indexer **Hilary Bird**

First published in the
United Kingdom in 2008
by Ryland Peters & Small
20–21 Jockey's Fields
London WC1R 4BW
www.rylandpeters.com

10 9 8 7 6 5 4 3 2 1

Text © Susannah Blake 2008
Design and commissioned photographs
© Ryland Peters & Small 2008

ISBN: 978-1-84597-725-2

A CIP record for this book is available from
the British Library.

Printed and bound in China.

Author's acknowledgements
Thank you to all my taste-testers for so
happily munching and accepting cakes at
every and any opportunity. But thank you
especially to Julie for advice and inspiration
when it comes to feeding teddy bears, and
to David for always looking so gleeful at the
prospect of another cake.

Contents

Introduction

The custom of afternoon tea is widely credited to Anna, the Duchess of Bedford, the wife of the seventh Duke of Bedford (1788–1861). At a time when meals took the form of a vast breakfast, followed by a light, picnic-style lunch and then a yawning gap until a late dinner in the evening, Anna proclaimed she had a 'sinking feeling' in the middle of the afternoon. To remedy this, she ordered cakes and tea at five o'clock. This delightful repast was soon picked up on and ladies would entertain, giving afternoon tea in turn.

The tradition of afternoon tea that we know and love became firmly established by the early nineteenth century, and Mrs Beeton described the meal in 1861 as '...tea and bread and butter, and a few elegant trifles in the way of cake and fruit.' Today, afternoon tea appears to be little changed, although perhaps the hotel teas enjoyed in London are somewhat more opulent and decadent than the meal's earlier incarnations. Tea is still served in a pot with milk or lemon, the bread and butter has evolved into dainty finger sandwiches or other savoury treats, and the elegant trifles include scones with clotted cream and jam, delicate sweet biscuits, large cakes and other fancies such as meringues and fruit-filled tartlets.

In today's health-conscious age, where time is of the essence, afternoon tea as a daily occurrence has fallen by the way-side, but it is seeing a resurgence in popularity as a way of entertaining. What could be a more charming and relaxing way to offer hospitality to your friends and loved ones than with a mid-afternoon feast? Taking time out from the hectic pace of life to sit back, relax, chat and enjoy each other's company? Afternoon tea is a civilized affair, without the stress or expenditure that a grand dinner party can entail. It has all the sophistication of smart entertaining, but in a relaxed environment – a meal of informal elegance that can be enjoyed in the cosy, relaxed environment of your sitting room or garden.

For this book, I have created twenty different tea party menus, each with their own distinctive character and charm. The menus draw not only on the traditional English afternoon tea, but look more widely to other tea traditions around the world – the Japanese tea ceremony that is so central to the Japanese culture and way of life, the Russian tea ceremony, Moroccan mint tea, and of course that classic refresher for all belles in the southern United States, iced tea. Each tea is a unique and individual affair, with a specific focus that means each menu will suit a different occasion, whether it's a tea party in the garden on a summer's afternoon, a birthday celebration for children or adults, a romantic tea for two, or a tea to enjoy in front of a roaring fire on a dark and wintry afternoon. Whichever tea party you choose, approach it with a sense of fun and *joie de vivre* – after all, it is a lighthearted meal and a frivolous decadence to be enjoyed with your dearest friends and loved ones.

Classic English Tea

Darjeeling

finger sandwiches

scones with clotted
cream and jam

butter cookies

lemon drizzle cake

That wonderful ritual of afternoon tea can take so many shapes

and forms, but the old-fashioned English tea – starting with finger

sandwiches and followed by scones spread with home-made jam

and clotted cream, golden, crumbly biscuits and a mouth-watering

slice of buttery, freshly baked cake – is hard to beat. The menu for

this classic tea draws on the absolute best of the afternoon tea

tradition, selecting the simplest, most delicious recipes to recreate

the quintessential English teatime experience.

finger sandwiches
Makes 12–16

A plateful of dainty little finger sandwiches, each one just a few mouthfuls, is the only way to begin a traditional afternoon tea. Classic fillings include thinly sliced cucumber or wafer-thin smoked salmon, but for a more sophisticated feel, try these irresistible fillings.

8 slices white or wholemeal bread
butter, at room temperature, for
  spreading

FOR THE PRAWN IN LEMON AND
CHILLI MAYONNAISE WITH ROCKET
2 tablespoons mayonnaise
1½ teaspoons sweet chilli sauce
1 teaspoon finely grated lemon zest
175 g cooked, peeled tiger prawns
a handful of wild rocket

FOR THE ARTICHOKE PÂTÉ WITH
SUN-BLUSH TOMATOES
400-g tin artichokes, drained
½ garlic clove
½ teaspoon ground coriander
1 tablespoon olive oil
85 g sun-blush tomatoes
a few fresh basil leaves, roughly torn
freshly ground black pepper

To make the prawn sandwiches, put the mayonnaise, sweet chilli sauce and lemon zest in a bowl and stir to combine. Add the prawns and gently fold together.

Thinly butter four slices of bread. Spread the prawn mixture on top of two of the slices, top with rocket and lay the other two slices of bread on top. To cut, put your hand on top of the sandwich and press down gently. Using a serrated knife and a gentle sawing motion, cut off the crusts. Next, cut the sandwich lengthways into three fingers.

To make the artichoke pâté, put the artichokes, garlic, coriander and olive oil in a food processor. Add a good grinding of black pepper and whizz until smooth.

Thinly butter the remaining four slices of bread. Spread two slices with the pâté. (Any left over can be stored in the fridge for a couple of days.) Top each sandwich with a few sun-blush tomatoes. Sprinkle with basil and top with the remaining slices of bread. Cut as previously described.

DARJEELING
Considered by many to be the 'champagne' of Indian teas, Darjeeling is the classic choice for afternoon tea. It is grown in the foothills of the Himalayas and the First Flush pickings make a light, flowery and highly aromatic drink that is considered to be among the finest of teas available. Second Flush pickings have a more developed, fruitier flavour but all Darjeelings are of excellent quality and produce finely flavoured tea.

scones with clotted cream and jam
Makes 10–12

Scones are an essential part of an English afternoon tea. They're always at their best when freshly baked and served split open and smothered in thick clotted cream and lashings of home-made jam.

225 g self-raising flour
1 teaspoon baking powder
2 tablespoons caster sugar
50 g butter
75 ml milk
1 egg
clotted cream and strawberry or other fruit jam,
   to serve
a 4.5-cm biscuit cutter

Preheat the oven to 220°C (425°F) Gas 7. Put the flour, baking powder and sugar in a food processor and pulse to combine. Add the butter and process for about 20 seconds, until the mixture resembles fine breadcrumbs. Tip the mixture into a large bowl and make a well in the centre.

Beat together the egg and milk and reserve 1 tablespoon of the mixture. Pour the remaining mixture into the flour and work in using a fork. Turn out on to a floured work surface and knead briefly to make a soft, smooth dough. (Work in a little more flour if the mixture is sticky.)

Pat out the dough to a thickness of about 2.5 cm and stamp out rounds using a biscuit cutter. Put the rounds on the prepared baking tray, spacing them slightly apart. Brush with the reserved egg and milk mixture and bake in the oven for about 8 minutes, until risen and golden. Transfer to a wire rack and let cool slightly. Serve split open and spread with clotted cream and jam.

butter biscuits
Makes about 12

Often it's the simplest recipes that are the best and it's hard to beat these crisp, buttery biscuits. If you want a little added indulgence, don't roll the biscuit dough in demerara sugar but leave it plain – then drizzle the baked biscuits with lines of plain chocolate and leave to set before serving.

85 g butter, at room temperature
40 g caster sugar
125 g plain flour
demerara sugar, to coat

Put the butter and sugar in a large bowl and beat until pale and creamy. Add the flour and stir, then work the mixture together with your hands to form a soft, smooth dough.

Roll the dough into a log about 12 cm long and 4 cm in diameter. Sprinkle a layer of demerara sugar on a piece of greaseproof paper and roll the dough in the sugar to coat. Wrap the log in clingfilm and chill for about 30 minutes, until firm. Meanwhile, preheat the oven to 160°C (325°F) Gas 3 and grease a baking tray.

Remove the dough from the fridge, trim off the ends and cut into slices 8 mm thick and place slightly apart on the prepared baking tray. Pat the edges of the biscuits into neat rounds or ovals. Bake for about 15 minutes until just beginning to turn brown. Leave to cool on the baking tray for a few minutes then transfer to a wire rack to cool.

lemon drizzle cake
Wonderfully old-fashioned and an absolute must for afternoon tea, this cake is drenched in a sharp, zesty syrup that gives it an irresistible tang. It's perfect with a cup of aromatic Darjeeling and refreshingly light in both texture and taste.

Afternoon tea is popular with visitors to London's top hotels, where they can enjoy this classic tradition in elegant surroundings.

175 g butter, at room temperature
175 g caster sugar
3 eggs
grated zest of 1 lemon
175 g self-raising flour, sifted

FOR THE LEMON SYRUP
grated zest and juice of 1½ lemons
125 g caster sugar
a 20-cm, loose-bottomed, square cake tin, greased and lined

Preheat the oven to 180°C (350°F) Gas 4. Put the butter and sugar in a large bowl and beat until pale and creamy. Beat in the eggs one at a time, then stir in the lemon zest and fold in the flour. Spoon the mixture into the prepared cake tin and level the top. Bake in the preheated oven for about 35 minutes, until the cake has risen and is golden. A skewer inserted in the centre should come out clean.

While the cake bakes, make the syrup. Put the lemon juice and sugar in a small saucepan and warm gently, stirring, until the sugar dissolves. Bring to the boil and boil for about 1 minute, then remove from the heat and stir in the grated lemon zest. Set aside until needed.

When the cake is ready, remove it from the oven and prick the top all over using a skewer. Pour the syrup over it and leave the cake to cool in the tin. Carefully unmould to serve.

Japanese Tea

green tea

omelette rolls with
spring onions

rice cakes wrapped in
red bean paste

green tea ice cream

When hosting a Japanese-styled tea party, it would be impossible
not to acknowledge the ancient tradition of the tea ceremony, which
is so important to Japanese culture, and the principles of which
should guide this tea party as well. However, it should also be
mentioned that although food is often eaten during the full Japanese
tea ceremony, the tea party I have created here does not follow the
same rules. Everything about this tea party should reflect the calm,
tranquillity and harmonious principles of the traditional tea ceremony.
The omelette rolls and cakes should be arranged beautifully on
platters, the ice cream served in delicate portions and the tea served
in small tea bowls.

THE JAPANESE TEA CEREMONY

Practised for hundreds of years, the tea ceremony has been strongly influenced by Zen Buddhism. The ritual interweaves the principles of harmony, respect, purity and tranquillity and offers a quiet interlude when the host and guests may strive for spiritual refreshment and harmony with the universe. A full tea ceremony involves a meal and two types of tea – thick and thin – and can last for up to four hours, but there are other shorter, simpler tea ceremonies as well. During the ceremony, matcha – or powdered green tea – is drunk. Guests kneel on mats facing their host, who carries out a series of ritualistic and prescribed movements such as lighting the charcoal brazier, and whisking the matcha and boiling water in a tea bowl. Each guest drinks from the same tea bowl, carefully wiping the edge of the bowl before passing it to the next guest.

The Japanese discovered the benefits of tea-drinking from the Chinese, the result of contact between Buddhist priests from the two countries.

omelette rolls with spring onions
Makes 12

This Japanese-style omelette looks stunning and makes the perfect savoury bite to serve before the sweet treats. Although it looks a little fiddly to make, it's actually very straightforward. Don't worry if your rolling technique is a little messy – all manner of mistakes can be rectified once the rolled omelette has been compressed inside the sushi-rolling mat.

6 eggs
4 tablespoons chopped spring onions, plus a few whole to garnish
4 tablespoons chicken or vegetable stock
2 tablespoons mirin (cooking sake)
1 teaspoon soy sauce
1 tablespoon caster sugar
salt and freshly ground black pepper
sunflower oil, for greasing
a sushi-rolling mat covered with a sheet of clingfilm

Put the eggs, chopped spring onions, stock, mirin, soy sauce and sugar in a bowl. Season with pepper and a pinch of salt and whisk to combine. Divide the mixture between two bowls.

Lightly grease an omelette pan using a piece of kitchen paper dampened with oil.

Take one of the bowls and pour about one-third of the egg mixture into the pan. Cook until almost set, then carefully roll up the omelette and nudge it to one side on the pan. Pour in half the remaining mixture and cook until almost set, then roll up the rolled omelette inside this fresh omelette and return to the side of the pan. Pour the remaining mixture into the pan and when nearly set, roll up the rolled omelettes in it in the same way.

Slide the omelette roll on to the sushi-rolling mat, roll up tightly and leave for at least 5 minutes. Repeat with the remaining bowl of mixture to make a second omelette roll.

Unroll the sushi mat, trim the ends of the omelette rolls and slice each one into six pieces. To garnish, cut the whole spring onions into thin strips. Tie a strip of spring onion around the centre of each piece of omelette roll. Serve warm or cold, as you prefer.

rice cakes wrapped in red bean paste
Makes 10

The Japanese make many different types of sweet rice cakes, but these, known as 'ohagi' are particularly popular and are often served to mark celebrations such as the arrival of new seasons. Although they are not difficult to make, you will need to remember to leave lots of time for soaking the beans and rice.

115 g dried aduki beans, soaked
   for 4 hours
115 g caster sugar
200 g sushi rice
sea salt
a scrupulously clean tea towel

Drain the beans, put them in a saucepan and pour sufficient water over them to cover. Bring to a rapid boil and boil for 10 minutes, then drain and rinse well. Return the beans to the pan, cover in plenty of water and bring to the boil. Reduce the heat and simmer for about 50 minutes until very soft. Add more water during cooking so that the beans are kept covered.

Add the sugar and a pinch of salt and stir to combine, then tip the mixture into a food processor or blender and blend to make a coarse purée, Return to the pan and simmer, stirring, for about 10 minutes or until the paste is thick. Remove from the heat and leave to cool.

Wash the rice several times until the water appears clear, then drain well and leave to dry for 1 hour. Put the rice in a pan, pour in 250 ml cold water, cover and bring to the boil. Reduce the heat and simmer for about 10 minutes, until all the water has been absorbed. Remove from the heat, cover and let stand for 10 minutes.

When the rice is cool enough to handle, shape it into about 10 balls. Soak a tea towel in cold water, then wring it out so that it feels damp. Spread about 1½ tablespoons of the bean paste in the centre of the cloth and put a rice ball in the centre. Gently wrap the paste around the ball. Repeat with the remaining paste and rice balls, putting the paste on a clean bit of cloth each time. Arrange on a plate to serve.

green tea ice cream
Makes about 1 litre

Delicately flavoured green tea ice cream is a favourite in Japan and a wonderful treat to serve at a Japanese-style tea party. Serve single, elegant scoops in pretty porcelain Japanese bowls. You can find matcha green tea powder in specialist Asian stores, larger supermarkets and it is available from many specialist internet retailers.

3 tablespoons matcha (powdered
   green tea)
3 tablespoons boiling water
350 ml full-fat milk
3 egg yolks
1 teaspoon cornflour
75 g caster sugar
400 ml double cream
an ice cream maker

Whisk together the matcha and boiling water, then transfer to a saucepan and add the milk. Set over medium heat and bring almost to the boil. Remove from the heat and let cool slightly.

Whisk the egg yolks, cornflour and sugar until thick and pale, then pour on to the hot milk mixture, whisking constantly. Return the pan to the heat and heat gently, stirring constantly, until thickened.

Pour the custard into a bowl, press clingfilm over the surface, then leave to cool. Stir the cream into the custard, then churn in an ice cream maker until thick. Scoop into dishes, or freeze until ready to serve.

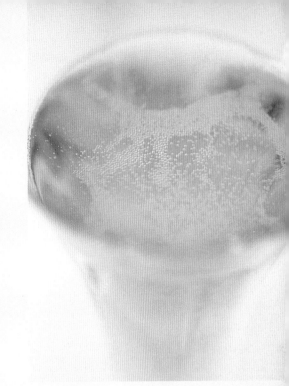

Champagne Tea

gunpowder green tea

elegant teatime crostini

orange and almond cake

strawberries and cream
with shortbread biscuits

Just mention fizz and people's eyes will sparkle in anticipation. A glass of frothy, chilled champagne is a classic addition to the ritual of afternoon tea and brings a sophisticated touch to what is already an elegant treat. Whether you choose non-vintage, vintage, dry, sweet or pink champagne is up to you, but a glass flute misted with condensation is a must. Strawberries have a natural affinity with champagne, so they are the obvious choice as the grand finale of this light and special menu. You can serve a champagne tea for any special occasion, but I think it's perfect in the summer months, when strawberries are in season and at their fragrant and juicy best.

GUNPOWDER GREEN TEA

Most gunpowder teas are made in Zhejiang province in China. They get their rather curious name from the fact that the tightly rolled 'pearls' of dried tea leaves resemble pellets of gunpowder. These little pellets gradually open in hot water to release their warm amber colour and produce a light and refreshing tea with a herby flavour. Taken without milk, gunpowder tea is the perfect choice for this champagne tea party, as it will not fight for attention with the fizz.

Serve your champagne in a fine, thin flute with a hollow stem or, for a more vintage feel, go for a traditional champagne saucer glass, also known as a coupe.

elegant teatime crostini
Makes 24

These crisp little toasts are very easy to make, yet look very impressive when arranged on a large serving platter. You can toast the bread and make the toppings in advance, then simply assemble the crostini just before serving.

FOR THE CROSTINI TOASTS
1 French-style baguette
olive oil, for brushing

Preheat the oven to 190°C (375°F) Gas 5. Cut 24 thin slices of baguette and lightly brush both sides of each one with oil. Arrange on a baking tray and bake for about 10 minutes, until crisp and golden. Transfer to a wire rack and let cool while you make the toppings.

FOR THE PEA AND PARMESAN TOPPING
2 tablespoons olive oil
2 shallots, finely chopped
200 g frozen peas
3 tablespoons dry white wine
dried chilli flakes, to taste (optional)
sea salt
Parmesan cheese shavings, to serve

Heat the oil in a saucepan set over low heat. Add the shallots and gently sauté for about 3 minutes, until tender and translucent. Add the peas and the wine to the pan. Cover and cook for 3 minutes, until the peas are tender, then tip them into a food processor or blender and whizz until smooth. Transfer to a bowl and season to taste with salt and a pinch of dried chilli flakes, if using.

To assemble the crostini, spoon the pea purée (either cold or warm, as liked) on to 12 crostini toasts, top with Parmesan shavings and serve immediately.

FOR THE SMOKED SALMON TOPPING
3 tablespoons mayonnaise
½ teaspoon finely grated zest from an unwaxed lemon
3–4 drops of Tabasco or other hot sauce, to taste
100 g smoked salmon, cut into 12 strips
½ lemon, for squeezing
freshly ground black pepper
fresh dill sprigs, to garnish

Combine the mayonnaise, lemon zest and Tabasco. To assemble the crostini, spoon a dollop of the lemon mayonnaise on to 12 crostini toasts. Top with a strip of smoked salmon and squeeze some lemon juice over it. Grind a little black pepper on top, garnish with a sprig of dill and serve immediately.

orange and almond cake
Serves 8

Dense, moist and zesty, this indulgent cake is perfect for a champagne tea. If you like, you could forego the shortbread biscuits (see right) and simply serve strawberries alongside a slice of this cake with a little dollop of whipped cream.

1 seedless orange
50 g ground almonds
175 g butter, at room temperature
175 g caster sugar
3 eggs
175 g self-raising flour
½ teaspoon bicarbonate of soda
icing sugar, for dusting
a 20-cm round (and at least 5.5 cm deep) cake tin, lined with greaseproof paper

Preheat the oven to 180°C (350°F) Gas 4. Finely grate the zest from the orange and set aside. Cut away the white pith from the orange and discard, leaving only the flesh. Put the flesh in a food processor or blender and whizz to make a purée. Add the ground almonds and blend briefly to make a smooth paste. Stir in the orange zest and set aside.

Put the butter and sugar in a large bowl and beat until pale and fluffy. Beat in the eggs one at a time. Combine the flour and bicarbonate of soda, sift into the egg mixture and fold it in. Add the orange and almond mixture and mix to combine. Spoon the mixture into the prepared cake tin and level the surface. Bake in the preheated oven for about 40 minutes, until the cake has risen and is golden. A skewer inserted in the centre should come out clean.

Leave to rest in the tin for 10 minutes, then turn out on to a wire rack to cool. Dust with icing sugar to serve.

strawberries and cream with shortbread biscuits

Serves 6

Sweet summer strawberries are the perfect partner for a glass of chilled fizz. Serve them with whipped cream and buttery shortbread biscuits for a real treat. Simply pile the strawberries in a bowl and let guests help themselves or, if you want to go for a more sophisticated presentation, serve the strawberries and cream layered between two shortbreads to create an elegant sandwich.

700 g strawberries, hulled and halved,
  (keep 3 unhulled to garnish)
1 tablespoon caster sugar
2 tablespoons orange-flavoured liqueur,
  such as Grand Marnier
whipped cream, to serve

FOR THE SHORTBREAD BISCUITS
Makes 12
115 g unsalted butter, at room temperature
60 g caster sugar, plus extra for sprinkling
180 g plain flour, sifted
icing sugar, for dusting

Preheat the oven to 170°C (340°F) Gas 3 and lightly grease a baking tray.

Put the butter and sugar in a large bowl and beat until pale and creamy. Add the flour and beat well to combine. Lightly knead the mixture until it comes together into a soft, pliable dough. Use your hands to shape the dough into a log measuring about 6–7 cm in diameter. Wrap the log in clingfilm and chill for 1–1½ hours until firm.

Meanwhile, put the strawberries in a bowl. Sprinkle with the sugar and add the orange-flavoured liqueur. Gently toss; cover and chill until you are ready to serve.

Cut the log into 12 slices, each about 5 mm thick. Arrange them on the prepared baking tray, sprinkle with a little sugar and bake in the preheated oven for about 14–15 minutes, until pale golden. Let rest on the baking tray for 2 minutes, then transfer to a wire rack to cool completely.

To assemble, spoon a little cream on to a biscuit, then top with a few strawberries and a second biscuit. Garnish with an unhulled strawberry half and dust with icing sugar. Repeat to create five more stacks. Serve immediately.

Mother's Day Tea

Earl Grey tea

finger sandwiches

lemon shortbread

Victoria sandwich cake

Although Mother's Day falls on different days in different countries, it's usually celebrated in spring or early summer, so the choice of food for this particular tea party menu reflects this, with light and refreshing flavours. The recipes are also wonderfully simple to follow and could be made by children under supervision so you're guaranteed a tasty spread that's also as pretty as a picture. Mother's Day is also the perfect excuse to decorate the table with beautiful, fragrant flowers freshly picked from the garden.

EARL GREY TEA

This popular flavoured tea is a blend of China black tea and essential oil of bergamot. Various stories have developed over the decades to explain its origin, the most popular being that it was specially blended for Earl Grey (British prime minister from 1830–1834) after a successful diplomatic mission to China. Whatever the origin of this famous blend, it is wonderfully aromatic and has a smoky yet citrusy flavour that is light and refreshing. It is best served black with a slice of lemon.

Breakfast in bed might be the traditional Mother's Day treat, but why not ring the changes and set out an attractive teatime spread on a table decorated with a vase of sweet-smelling flowers.

finger sandwiches
Makes 12–16

Egg mayonnaise with peppery watercress is a classic teatime finger sandwich filling. Brie and cranberry jelly is less traditional, but no less delicious! For more ideas for fillings, see page 10.

8 slices white or wholemeal bread
butter, at room temperature, for
    spreading
salt and freshly ground black pepper

FOR THE EGG MAYONNAISE AND
WATERCRESS FILLING
2 tablespoons mayonnaise
½ teaspoon Dijon mustard
2 hard-boiled eggs, cooled
a handful of watercress

FOR THE BRIE AND CRANBERRY
FILLING
115 g Brie or Camembert, at room
temperature
1–1½ tablespoons cranberry jelly

To make the egg sandwiches, thinly butter four slices of bread. Put the mayonnaise and mustard in a small bowl and stir to combine. Peel the eggs, put them in a separate bowl and mash well with a fork. Add the mayonnaise to the eggs and mash again until the whites have broken up and the mixture is creamy. Season to taste with salt and pepper. Divide the mixture between two slices of bread and spread evenly. Top each with watercress and a second slice of bread. To cut, put your hand on top of the sandwich and press down gently. Using a serrated knife and a gentle sawing motion, cut off the crusts. Cut the sandwich lengthways into three fingers.

To make the Brie and cranberry sandwiches, thinly butter four slices of bread. Spread two slices with cranberry jelly. Cut the Brie into thin slices and arrange them on top. Season to taste with pepper and top with a slice of bread. Using a serrated knife and a gentle sawing motion, cut off the crusts. Cut the sandwich lengthways into three fingers.

lemon shortbread
Makes 16

A deliciously buttery shortbread with a tangy, lemony topping.

175 g plain flour
115 g butter, diced
50 g caster sugar

FOR THE LEMON TOPPING
2 eggs
3 tablespoons plain flour
grated zest and freshly squeezed
    juice of 1 unwaxed lemon
60 ml crème fraîche
115 g caster sugar
lemon slices, to garnish (optional)
a 20-cm square cake tin, lined

Preheat the oven to 180°C (350°F) Gas 4. Put the flour and butter in a large bowl and use your fingertips to rub them together until the mixture resembles fine breadcrumbs. Add the sugar and work the mixture until it forms a soft, pliable dough. Press into the base of the prepared tin in an even layer, then prick the base all over using a fork. Bake in the preheated oven for 15 minutes, until lightly golden.

Meanwhile, crack one egg into a bowl, add the flour and beat until smooth. Beat in the second egg, then add the lemon zest and juice, crème fraîche and sugar, and whisk until smooth.

Remove the shortbread from the oven, pour over the lemon mixture, then return it to the oven and bake for a further 10 minutes until the topping has just set. Remove from the oven and let cool completely in the tin before cutting into 16 squares or diamonds, as preferred. Garnish with a slice of fresh lemon as shown, if liked.

Victoria sandwich cake
Serves 8

It's hard to beat a freshly baked, golden, buttery Victoria sponge filled with fresh raspberries and cream. If you prefer, you can use other red berries such as strawberries or blueberries, together with the equivalent jam.

180 g butter, at room temperature
180 g caster sugar
3 eggs
180 g self-raising flour
3½ tablespoons good-quality
    raspberry jam
140 g fresh raspberries
120 ml whipping cream
icing sugar, for dusting
*2 x 20-cm sandwich tins, greased
    and base-lined*

Preheat the oven to 180°C (350°F) Gas 4.

Put the butter and sugar in a bowl and beat together until pale and fluffy. Beat in the eggs one at a time. Sift in the flour and mix to combine.

Spoon the cake mixture into the prepared tins and level the surface using the back of the spoon. Bake in the preheated oven for 20–25 minutes until golden brown and the centre of the sponge springs back when lightly pressed. Turn the cakes out on to a wire rack, gently peel off the lining paper and leave to cool completely.

To serve, spread the jam over one cake and top with the raspberries. Whip the cream until it stands in soft peaks, then spread it over the raspberries. Put the second cake on top and dust with icing sugar.

Winter Wonderland

spiced Christmas tea

blue cheese and
pear crostini

white chocolate and
cranberry florentines

spiced star cookies

snow-topped coconut cake

When it's cold and frosty outside and the nights are drawing in,

there's no better time to stay indoors and enjoy a silvery-white winter

tea party. If you are holding it at Christmas you can really go to town

with the decorations – why not dress the table with sprigs of silver

foliage and vases of baubles, and hang sparkly fairy lights around the

room to create a fairy-tale wonderland that both children and adults

will adore? The menu is full of the traditional flavours and warming

spices that we associate with the festive season, and the gorgeous

star-shaped iced cookies and beautiful snowy-white coconut cake

make a sumptuous teatime display.

spiced Christmas tea
Serves 4

1 orange
1 lemon
4 teaspoons Darjeeling, or other
  lightly flavoured tea
1 cinnamon stick
3 cloves
4 juniper berries, lightly crushed
clear honey, to serve (optional)

Pour a few inches of boiling water into the bottom of a teapot and leave it to warm. Meanwhile, use a vegetable peeler to pare off a strip of rind from around the orange. Next, pare off three strips of rind from the lemon.

Fill the kettle with water and bring to the boil. Meanwhile, drain the water from the teapot and add the tea leaves, cinnamon, cloves, juniper berries and citrus rind. Pour freshly boiled water in and leave to infuse for 3–5 minutes until brewed to your taste. Serve sweetened with honey, if liked.

SPICED CHRISTMAS TEA
This delicious, subtly spiced brew is Darjeeling tea flavoured with citrus zest, cinnamon, juniper berries and cloves. Serve it black, sweetened with just a little honey. It makes a lovely non-alcoholic alternative to the mulled red wine that is so popular during the winter months.

Why not host a winter wonderland tea party every year and make it a keenly anticipated festive tradition for your friends or family?

blue cheese and pear crostini
Makes 12

Creamy, piquant Gorgonzola and sweet, juicy pear are a perfect pairing on these crisp, bite-sized crostini.

½ a French baguette
olive oil, for brushing
100 g Gorgonzola cheese
1 pear, peeled, halved, cored and cut into 12 thin wedges
12 walnut halves (optional)

Cut 12 thin slices from the baguette – they should be no more than 1 cm thick. Brush each one with a little oil then toast under a preheated grill until crisp and golden on both sides. Let cool.

When ready to serve, top each crostini with a pear wedge, a thin slice of Gorgonzola and a walnut half (if using).

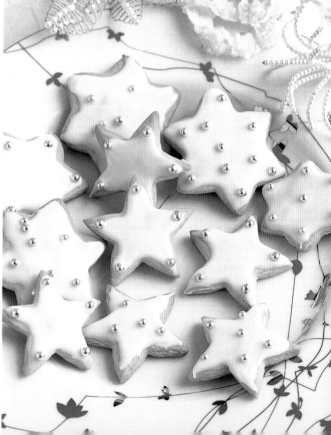

white chocolate and cranberry florentines

Makes about 24

Perfect little bites, just the right size for balancing on a saucer!

50 g butter
50 g caster sugar
3 tablespoons double cream
25 g flaked almonds
75 g mixed nuts, roughly chopped
4 glacé cherries, roughly chopped
40 g mixed peel, roughly chopped
15 g dried cranberries
25 g plain flour
100 g white chocolate, broken into
    small pieces
2 baking trays, lined with
    greaseproof paper and greased

Preheat the oven to 180°C (250°F) Gas 4. Put the butter, sugar and cream in a saucepan and set over low heat. Gently stir until melted, then bring to the boil. Remove from the heat and stir in the nuts, glacé cherries, mixed peel, cranberries and flour, and mix to combine. Drop teaspoonfuls of the mixture on the prepared baking trays, spacing them well apart. Bake in the preheated oven for about 10 minutes until golden, then remove from the oven and gently press the edges, using a palette knife, to form neat rounds. Leave to cool on the baking trays for about 10 minutes until firm, then carefully peel off the greaseproof paper and transfer the florentines to a wire rack to cool completely.

Put the white chocolate in a heatproof bowl and set it over a pan of simmering water. Stir it as it melts and let cool. Spread the underside of each florentine with a layer of white chocolate, then leave to firm up slightly before using the tines of a fork to make wavy lines in the chocolate. Leave to set.

spiced star cookies

Makes about 30

Nothing says Christmas to me like the smell of these cookies.

125 g unsalted butter, at room
    temperature
125 g sugar
125 g golden syrup
1 egg
1 teaspoon ground ginger
400 g self-raising flour
125 g icing sugar, sifted
4–5 teaspoons freshly squeezed
    lemon juice
edible silver balls, to decorate
2 baking trays, lightly greased
star-shaped cookie cutters of
    various sizes

Put the butter and sugar in a large bowl and beat until light and fluffy. Add the golden syrup, egg and ginger and beat again until well combined. Gradually sift in the flour, folding it in as you go. Tip the mixture on to a work surface and knead for about 5 minutes, until smooth. Wrap the dough in clingfilm and chill for at least 30 minutes.

Preheat the oven to 180°C (350°F) Gas 4. Roll out the dough on a lightly floured surface. Use the cookie cutters to stamp out star shapes. Carefully transfer them to the prepared baking trays. Press together any trimmings and re-roll to make more cookies.

Bake the cookies in the preheated oven for 10–12 minutes, until golden. Transfer them to a wire rack to cool.

Put the icing sugar in a small bowl, add a little lemon juice and stir until smooth. If the icing is too thick, add a drop more lemon juice. Spoon a little icing into the centre of each cookie and spread it out towards the edges using the tip of the spoon. Sprinkle with a few silver balls and leave to set before serving.

snow-topped coconut cake
Serves 6–8

This light, creamy cake has a refreshing kick of lime and makes a pretty alternative to a traditional Christmas cake.

40 g creamed coconut
140 g unsalted butter
175 g caster sugar
3 eggs
150 g self-raising flour
40 g desiccated coconut
grated zest of 1 unwaxed lime

FOR THE FROSTING
225 g cream cheese
75 g icing sugar
1 tablespoon freshly squeezed lime juice
40 g coconut chips
2 x 20-cm sandwich tins, greased and base-lined

Preheat the oven to 180°C (350°F) Gas 4. Put the creamed coconut in a bowl and soften with a wooden spoon. Add the butter and sugar and beat together until pale and fluffy. Beat in the eggs, one at a time. Sift in the flour and fold it in, then stir in the desiccated coconut and lime zest. Spoon the cake mixture into the prepared tins and level the surface using the back of a large metal spoon. Bake in the preheated oven for 20–25 minutes, until golden brown and a skewer inserted in the centre comes out clean. Turn the cakes out on to a wire rack, peel off the lining paper and let cool.

Beat together the cream cheese, icing sugar and lime juice. Place one of the cakes on a serving plate. Spread slightly less than half of the frosting on top of the cake, then place the second cake on top. Spread the remaining frosting over it and scatter with coconut chips to finish.

Valentine's Day Tea

jasmine tea

chilled vintage champagne

oysters with red wine and
shallot vinaigrette

spiced sugar palmiers

Valentine meringues

sticky dark chocolate
éclairs

What could be more romantic than tea for two? While the tradition on Valentine's day is often an intimate dinner, a late afternoon tea, prepared with love and served in glorious seclusion in a cushioned salon is a truly thoughtful gesture. Put a bottle of champagne on ice, set the table with candles to provide an atmospheric glow and fill a vase with scented roses. The menu for this tea is a perfect combination of sensuous indulgence, nostalgic romance and foodie heaven, all designed to ensure that your lover is left in no doubt at all about how you truly feel.

JASMINE TEA

This sweet, smooth Chinese tea with a delicate floral flavour and aroma is the perfect brew to serve with this luxurious menu. Jasmine flowers are gathered during the day and then stored in a cool place until night, when they open and release their powerful scent. The flowers are then layered between the green tea leaves and left to permeate them with their heady aroma. The following morning the spent flowers are removed, leaving only the jasmine-scented tea leaves. Jasmine tea should be enjoyed without milk.

oysters with red wine and shallot vinaigrette
Serves 2

One of life's luxuries, oysters are a sensual pleasure and have been revered as an aphrodisiac for centuries. The age-old rule that oysters should be bought when there is an 'r' in the month means that they are the perfect choice for February 14th.

6 fresh oysters, well scrubbed
½ shallot, very finely diced
3 tablespoons red wine vinegar
crushed ice, to serve
an oyster knife (optional)

Wrap a tea towel around your hand to protect it, then hold an oyster flat-side up. Slide an oyster knife (or a knife with a short, blunt blade) into the hinge and gently wiggle it back and forth to prise the shell open. Discard the upper shell, then slide the knife under the oyster to release it from the lower shell. Repeat with the remaining oysters. Return them to the lower shells and arrange on a serving plate full of crushed ice. Combine the diced shallot and vinegar in a small bowl, then drizzle a little over each oyster. Serve immediately.

spiced sugar palmiers
Makes 12

Incredibly simple to make and delectable to eat, these light, heart-shaped pastries are perfect for a Valentine's tea.

175 g ready-made puff pastry, thawed if frozen
2 tablespoons caster sugar
¼ teaspoon ground cinnamon

Preheat the oven to 200°C (400°F) Gas 6. Roll out the pastry on a lightly floured surface to a thickness of about 5 mm. Trim it to a neat 24 cm x 14 cm rectangle. Combine the sugar and cinnamon and sprinkle three-quarters of it over the pastry in an even layer.

Starting from one short end, roll up the pastry until you reach the middle, then repeat from the other end. Trim the ends neatly, then cut into slices 1 cm thick.

Arrange the slices on a lightly greased baking tray, patting them into shape if necessary. Sprinkle with the remaining cinnamon sugar and bake in the preheated oven for about 12 minutes, until risen and golden. Remove from the oven and transfer to a wire rack to cool completely.

Valentine meringues
Makes about 20

These tiny, pale pink meringues with their melt-in-the-mouth texture are ideal for a Valentine's day tea. Serve them piled up on a plate – just as they are – or sandwich them together with whipped cream.

2 small or 1 large egg white
60 g caster sugar
a few drops of red food colouring
whipped cream, to serve (optional)
2 baking trays, covered with baking parchment

Preheat the oven to 110°C (225°F) Gas ¼.

Put the egg white in a clean, grease-free bowl and whisk until soft peaks form. Whisk in the sugar, one tablespoon at a time, until the meringue is thick and glossy. Add a few drops of red food colouring with the last tablespoon of sugar to achieve a pretty rose pink.

Dollop teaspoonfuls of the meringue mixture on the prepared baking trays, spacing them well apart, and bake in the preheated oven for about 1¼ hours until crisp. Turn off the oven and leave the meringues in the oven to cool. Serve plain or sandwiched together with a little whipped cream.

Small, bite-sized treats that you can eat with your fingers add to the sensuality of this Valentine's tea, making it perfect for a romantic lover's tryst.

sticky dark chocolate éclairs

Makes about 20

There's something wickedly indulgent about chocolate éclairs and these bite-sized ones covered with a rich, dark chocolate sauce and oozing with freshly whipped cream do not disappoint! If you're feeling particularly naughty, don't even bother with a fork and just pick them up in your fingers, then lick off the mess!

75 g plain flour
60 ml milk
50 g chilled butter, diced
a pinch of salt
2 eggs
125 ml double cream, whipped
2 baking trays lined with
   greaseproof paper
a piping bag, fitted with
   a 1–1.5-cm nozzle

FOR THE CHOCOLATE SAUCE
125 g dark chocolate, chopped
125 ml double cream

Preheat the oven to 220°C (425°F) Gas 7. Sift the flour on to a sheet of greaseproof paper. Put the milk, 60 ml cold water, butter and salt into a saucepan and bring to the boil. Let boil for 1 minute then remove from the heat and tip the flour into the pan. Beat until the mixture is just smooth and then return the pan to the heat and cook, stirring constantly, for about 1 minute. Remove the pan from the heat and beat in the eggs, one at a time, until the mixture forms a smooth and glossy paste.

Spoon the mixture into the piping bag and pipe 20 small fingers, each about 5–6 cm long, on the prepared baking trays. Bake in the preheated oven for about 12 minutes, until golden. Transfer to a wire rack. Use a sharp knife to cut a slit in the side of each éclair. Let cool completely while you make the chocolate sauce.

Put the chocolate and cream in a bowl set over a pan of gently simmering water and heat gently until the chocolate is almost melted. Stir until melted and the mixture is smooth. Use a teaspoon to gently fill each éclair with a little whipped cream. Spoon some chocolate sauce over each one and serve as soon as possible.

Baby Shower

lime blossom or
rosehip tea

creamy tomato and
mascarpone tartlets with
chargrilled artichokes

baby boy and girl
flower cookies

spiced carrot and
pistachio cake

white chocolate and
lemon truffle balls

Every expectant mother deserves a baby shower a month or

so before the arrival of her new baby. It's an exciting time, and a

wonderful excuse to bring together all her girlfriends for a last bit

of pampering and indulgence before those sleepless nights begin!

A tea party is the perfect choice for the occasion – easier to work

into your guests' schedules than an evening, especially if they have

small children themselves. Set the table with pastel linens for a

delicate, nursery feel and do make sure that the mum-to-be has

a suitably comfortable chair in which to sit, as she opens her gifts

and enjoys being the centre of attention.

LIME BLOSSOM
OR ROSEHIP TEAS

For a baby shower, it is best to choose a caffeine-free tea as so many expectant mothers eliminate or try to cut down on caffeine during pregnancy. That said, certain types of herbal teas are best avoided by pregnant women because of their unwelcome therapeutic qualities. Fruity infusions such as rosehip or refreshing lime blossom, are safe to drink at any stage during pregnancy, and will complement the foods in this light menu.

baby boy and girl flower cookies
Makes 20

These cute, flower-shaped sugar cookies with pink and blue icing couldn't be simpler to make and taste divine.

150 g plain flour
85 g chilled butter, diced
60 g caster sugar
1 egg yolk
2 baking trays, lightly greased
a flower-shaped cookie cutter,
  6 cm in diameter

TO DECORATE
100 g icing sugar, sifted
1 tablespoon freshly squeezed
  lemon juice
red and blue food colouring

Put the flour and butter in a food processor and process until the mixture resembles breadcrumbs. Add the sugar and egg yolk and whizz until the mixture starts to come together. Turn the mixture out on to a clean work surface and knead gently to form a soft dough. Shape the dough into a ball, wrap in clingfilm and chill for 30 minutes.

Preheat the oven to 180°C (350°F) Gas 4.

Roll out the dough on a lightly floured work surface, to a thickness of about 4 mm. Use the cookie cutter to stamp out flower shapes and lift them on to the prepared baking trays. Re-roll the trimmings to make more cookies.

Bake in the preheated oven for about 12 minutes, until pale golden. Transfer to a wire rack and let cool completely before icing them.

Put the icing sugar in a bowl with the lemon juice and stir until smooth. Spoon half of the icing into a separate bowl. Tint one batch of icing pink with a drop of red food colouring, and add a drop of blue food colouring to the other batch.

Spoon a circle of blue icing in the centre of half the flowers, and a circle of pink icing in the centre of the remaining flowers. Leave to set before serving.

creamy tomato and mascarpone tartlets with chargrilled artichokes

Makes 12

These pretty little tartlets make a lovely savoury. You can prepare the tartlet cases and filling in advance, then simply assemble the tarts at the last minute. For a winter baby shower, you can serve the tartlets warm by simply warming through the filling before spooning into the freshly baked pastry cases.

FOR THE TARTLET CASES
85 g plain flour
40 g chilled butter, diced
40 g Parmesan cheese, finely grated
a biscuit cutter, 6.5 cm in diameter
a 12-cup, non-stick, mini tartlet tin

FOR THE FILLING
1½ tablespoons olive oil
1 garlic clove, finely chopped
1 large red pepper, deseeded and chopped
1½ tablespoons mascarpone cheese
½ teaspoon cider vinegar
½ handful fresh basil leaves, chopped,
   plus a few extra to garnish
2 marinated artichoke hearts, drained
sea salt and freshly ground black pepper

To make the pastry, put the flour, butter and Parmesan in a food processor and process until the mixture resembles fine breadcrumbs. Gradually add about 1 tablespoon iced water until the mixture comes together. Shape into a ball, wrap in clingfilm and chill for 1 hour.

To make the filling, gently fry the garlic and pepper in the oil for 20 minutes until soft, then tip into a food processor and blend until smooth. Transfer the mixture to a bowl, and stir in the mascarpone cheese, vinegar and chopped basil. Season to taste, cover and set aside.

Preheat the oven to 190°C (350°F) Gas 5. Roll out the pastry on a lightly floured surface and cut out 12 rounds using the biscuit cutter. Press the rounds into the tartlet tin and prick the base of each with a fork. Bake in the preheated oven for about 12 minutes, until crisp and golden. Transfer to a wire rack to cool.

To serve, cut each artichoke heart into six wedges. Spoon a little red pepper mixture into each tartlet case, top with artichoke and grind a little black pepper on top to serve.

spiced carrot and pistachio cake
Serves 8

There's something comforting and homely about carrot cake, making it the perfect indulgent centrepiece for this cosy baby shower tea. This one has a lemony cream cheese frosting and a dense, moist crumb.

225 g self-raising flour
1 teaspoon baking powder
1 teaspoon ground cinnnamon
½ teaspoon ground ginger
¼ teaspoon freshly grated nutmeg
150 ml sunflower oil
3 eggs
200 g soft light brown sugar
350 g grated carrot
grated zest of 1 unwaxed orange
60 g roasted, unsalted pistachio
    nuts, roughly chopped
*a 20-cm cake tin, greased and
    lined with greaseproof paper*

FOR THE FROSTING AND TO DECORATE
200 g cream cheese
75 g icing sugar
1½ teaspoons lemon juice
grated zest of 1 lemon
chopped unsalted pistachio nuts
crystallized violet and/or rose petals

Preheat the oven to 180°C (350°F) Gas 4.

Sift the flour, baking powder and spices into a large bowl and make a well in the centre. In a separate bowl, beat together the oil, eggs and sugar. Pour this mixture into the dry ingredients and fold together. Add the grated carrot, orange zest and nuts and mix.

Spoon the mixture into the prepared cake tin, level out the surface and bake in the preheated oven for about 1 hour, or until a skewer inserted in the centre comes out clean. Leave to cool in the tin for 10 minutes, then turn out on to a wire rack to cool.

To make the frosting, beat together the cream cheese, icing sugar, lemon juice and zest until smooth and creamy. Spread over the cooled cake, then decorate with pistachios and crystallized petals.

white chocolate and lemon truffle balls
Makes about 14

These buttery truffle balls flavoured with lemon zest are a lovely treat. They can be made in advance and chilled until ready to serve.

100 g white chocolate
50 g butter
2 tablespoons double cream
¾ teaspoon grated lemon zest
115 g Madeira cake, finely crumbled
mini muffin or petit four cases

TO DECORATE
50 g white chocolate
icing sugar, for dusting

Break the white chocolate into a heatproof bowl, add the butter and set over a pan of gently simmering water until melted. Remove from the heat, add the cream and continue stirring until the mixture is smooth and

creamy. Stir in the lemon zest, followed by the cake crumbs.

Take spoonfuls of the mixture and use your fingers to roll them into walnut-sized balls. Place the balls in the paper cases and chill for at least 2 hours, until firm.

To decorate, melt the remaining chocolate in a bowl set over a pan of gently simmering water. Dip a skewer into the melted chocolate and drizzle zigzags of chocolate over the truffle balls. Chill until the chocolate has set. Dust lightly with icing sugar just before serving.

French Tea

Formosa oolong tea

mini croque-monsieurs

macaroons

raspberry and lemon
mille-feuilles

strawberry sablés

A French tea party should be the height of sophistication. You may not have access to a chic boudoir filled with Louis XIV furniture but you can create a feeling of refinement and elegance by laying out crisp white linen napkins, beautiful china and any silverware that you might have. If you have dainty little cake forks this is the perfect opportunity to use them. Every morsel of food is presented in delicate, bite-sized portions designed to tantalize, titillate and flirt with the taste buds. There should be no slabs of cake or scones slathered with cream at a French tea party – it's high style, sophistication and elegance every step of the way!

FORMOSA OOLONG

Oolong teas are semi-oxidized and vary in style from a light, floral liquor to dark brown leafed teas with an earthier flavour. Formosa oolong comes specifically from Taiwan – formally known as Formosa. The long twisted leaves, which are a mix of brown, black and dark red with hints of green and silver, brew to make a bright, golden tea. It has a remarkable flavour, reminiscent of fresh peaches and apricots with just a hint of spice and there is no astringency or bitterness. And it is this distinctive and rather sophisticated flavour that seems to make it so perfect for a French-style tea party. Sip it without milk, as you nibble on the tasty French savouries and pastries in this menu.

In France, the salon de thé is an institution. Highly skilled pâtissiers are masters of their art, creating breathtaking displays of cakes and macaroons in a myriad of colours.

mini croque-monsieurs
Makes 12

Crisp croque-monsieur sandwiches, oozing with melting Gruyère and ham, are a favourite in French cafes. These amusing miniature versions are the perfect savoury to serve at the beginning of a French-style tea party. They're simple to make and you could even prepare them ahead of time, ready to toast when your guests arrive.

a French-style baguette
2 teaspoons Dijon mustard
115 g Gruyère cheese, grated
85 g prosciutto or other ham
butter, at room temperature
chopped flat-leaf parsley, to garnish
freshly ground black pepper

Cut 24 thin slices of baguette, each about about 7 mm thick. Spread half the slices with mustard, then top with half the cheese and put a piece of prosciutto on top. Top with the remaining slices of bread.

Preheat the grill to high. Lightly butter the sandwiches on both sides, then arrange them on a grill pan. Grill until golden, then turn over and grill until just golden on the second side. Sprinkle with the remaining cheese and grill for 1 minute, or until the cheese is melted and bubbling. Sprinkle with parsley and grind some black pepper over them to serve.

macaroons
Makes about 16

Little almond macaroons sandwiched together with fruit jam are a French classic and perfect for this sophisticated tea party. They will leave you plenty of room to indulge in the other delectable morsels on offer.

2 egg whites
115 g ground almonds
115 g icing sugar
blackcurrant jam, to serve
2 baking trays, lined with greaseproof paper
a piping bag

Preheat the oven to 180°C (350°F) Gas 4. Put the egg whites in a clean, grease-free bowl and whisk until stiff peaks form. Combine the almonds and icing sugar in a separate bowl, then sift into the egg whites and gently fold together until combined. Spoon the mixture into a piping bag and pipe 32 2-cm rounds on the prepared baking trays.

Bake in the preheated oven for about 10 minutes, until a light golden colour. Let cool slightly on the baking trays, then use a palette knife to carefully transfer to a wire rack to cool completely.

To assemble, spread half the macaroons with jam and sandwich them together with the remaining macaroons.

raspberry and lemon 'mille-feuilles'
Makes 8

For me, nothing beats the experience of breaking through the crisp pastry layers of a mille-feuille to reach the sweet cream and fruit layered within. This simplified version of the classic French pâtisserie is quick and easy to put together, yet looks utterly sophisticated and tastes divine.

250 g ready-made puff pastry,
    thawed if frozen
5 tablespoons lemon curd
300 ml crème fraîche
400 g fresh raspberries
icing sugar, to dust

Preheat the oven to 200°C (400°F) Gas 6.

Roll out the pastry to a thickness of 5 mm, then trim it to a 30 cm x 15 cm rectangle. Slice the pastry into 8 squares of equal size and arrange them on a lightly greased baking tray. Bake in the preheated oven for about 10 minutes, until puffed up and golden. Transfer to a wire rack to cool.

Once cool, use a serrated knife to carefully cut each pastry square in half horizontally to create 16 pieces. When ready to assemble the mille-feuilles, arrange eight of the pastry rectangles on a serving platter. Fold the lemon curd into the crème fraîche and spread about 2 tablespoons of the lemon cream on top of each one. Top with raspberries and a second pastry rectangle. Dust with icing sugar and serve immediately.

strawberry sablés

Makes about 30 biscuits

These very simple almond biscuits are a French classic and make a lovely contrast to the creamy indulgence of the mille-feuilles and the richness of the macaroons. It you prefer, you can simply serve them plain, rather than stacking them with strawberries – but it does add to that lovely feel of French sophistication.

225 g plain flour
50 g ground almonds
a pinch of salt
75 g icing sugar
130 g unsalted butter, diced
1 egg plus extra beaten egg for glazing
½ teaspoon vanilla extract
225 g very small strawberries
icing sugar, for dusting
2 baking trays, lined with greaseproof paper
a round biscuit cutter, 6 cm in diameter, ideally
*   with fluted edges*

Put the flour, almonds, salt and sugar in a food processor and pulse briefly to combine. Add the butter and pulse until the mixture resembles fine breadcrumbs. Beat together the egg and vanilla, then, with the machine still running, add the egg and process until the mixture just starts to come together and form a dough. Shape the dough into a ball, wrap it in clingfilm and chill for at least 1 hour.

Preheat the oven to 180°C (350°F) Gas 4. Roll out the dough on a lightly floured surface to a thickness of about 5 mm, then use the biscuit cutter to stamp out rounds. Re-roll any trimmings to make more rounds.

Arrange the rounds of dough on the prepared baking trays. Prick each one a few times with the tines of a fork, and brush with a little of the beaten egg. Bake in the preheated oven for about 15 minutes, until golden brown. Transfer to a wire rack to cool completely.

When ready to assemble, place three strawberries on half the biscuits, then top with the remaining biscuits. Dust liberally with icing sugar and serve immediately. Alternatively, serve the strawberries in small glass bowls with the sablés on the side.

Floral Garden Tea

Keemun tea

rosemary scones with
cream cheese and
Parma ham

lavender shortbread

dark chocolate floral cake

meringues with
rosewater cream

Summer afternoons, when gardens are in full bloom, are made for

serving this floral-inspired afternoon tea. Arrange a table and chairs

in a shady area of your garden. If you don't have trees to provide

dappled shade, try setting up a parasol or canopy to protect

your guests from the sun. Relax and enjoy this delicious menu of

rosemary-scented scones, shortbread redolent with the delicate

flavour of lavender, meringues sandwiched with rosewater cream and

a rich chocolate cake scattered with pretty, crystallized violet petals.

Simply heavenly.

KEEMUN TEA

This classic, black china tea has a lightly scented, almost nutty, smooth flavour with a delicate aroma and natural sweetness. It's light and refreshing, making it perfect for this pretty garden party tea and – depending on the strength of the brew – it is delicious served either black or with milk. My preference is for a lightly brewed cup without milk, to let the subtle floral flavours of the scones, shortbread and cake shine through.

rosemary scones with cream cheese and Parma ham
Makes 12

Rosemary has a wonderfully intense aroma and flavour. These savoury scones are topped with creamy cheese and strips of Parma ham – its saltiness offset by the sweet, juicy grapes. Delicious.

225 g self-raising flour
1 teaspoon baking powder
¼ teaspoon salt
2 teaspoons chopped fresh rosemary
50 g butter
100 ml full-fat milk
1 egg
150 g cream cheese
85 g thinly sliced Parma ham
100 g seedless grapes, halved
a biscuit cutter, 4–5 cm in diameter

Preheat the oven to 220°C (425°F) Gas 7. Put the flour, baking powder, salt and rosemary in a food processor and pulse to combine. Add the butter and process for about 20 seconds until the mixture resembles fine breadcrumbs. Tip into a large bowl and make a well in the middle.

Beat together the egg and milk, then reserve 1 tablespoon of the mixture. Pour the remaining mixture into the flour and work it in using a fork. Turn out on to a floured surface and knead briefly to make a soft, smooth dough. (Work in a little more flour if the mixture is sticky.)

Roll or pat out the dough to a thickness of about 2.5 cm and stamp out 12 rounds with the biscuit cutter. Arrange them on a greased baking tray, spacing them slightly apart, and brush with the reserved egg and milk mixture. Bake in the preheated oven for about 8 minutes until risen and golden, then transfer to a wire rack to cool. Serve spread with cream cheese and topped with Parma ham and halved grapes.

lavender shortbread
Makes 18

These crisp, buttery shortbreads are subtly scented with the delicate flavour of lavender and have a timeless elegance that makes them absolutely perfect for the traditional garden setting of this tea.

50 g caster sugar, plus extra for sprinkling
⅓ teaspoon dried lavender flowers
175 g plain flour
115 g unsalted butter, chilled and diced
a few sprigs of fresh lavender, to decorate
  (optional)
an 18-cm square cake tin, greased and lined

Preheat the oven to 160°C (325°F) Gas 3. Put the sugar and dried lavender flowers in a food processor and pulse briefly until the flowers are just chopped. Set aside.

Put the flour and butter in a bowl and work together with your fingertips until the mixture resembles fine breadcrumbs. Add the lavender and sugar mixture and stir to combine, then use your hands to work the mixture into a dough.

Press the dough into the base of the prepared tin, pressing it flat using the base of a glass. Prick the surface all over using the tines of a fork, then use a sharp knife to score into 18 fingers. Sprinkle the shortbread lightly with sugar, then bake in the preheated oven for about 35–40 minutes, until a pale straw colour.

Cut into fingers along the scored lines and let cool in the tin. Decorate with fresh lavender flowers, if using, to serve.

A garden in full bloom on a summer's afternoon is the perfect venue for this delightfully pretty and perfumed tea party.

dark chocolate floral cake

Serves 8–12

A crumbly chocolate cake covered in rich, glossy frosting and decorated with crystallized flower petals makes a stunning centrepiece for this garden tea party. Serve it just as it is, or with chilled whipped cream on the side.

100 g plain chocolate
125 g butter, at room temperature
170 g caster sugar
2 eggs, separated
170 g self-raising flour
1 tablespoon unsweetened cocoa powder
60 ml full-fat milk
a 20-cm springform cake tin, greased and base-lined

FROSTING AND TO DECORATE
200 g plain chocolate, chopped
200 ml double cream
crystallized violets

Preheat the oven to 180°C (350°F) Gas 4. Put the chocolate in a heatproof bowl and set over a pan of barely simmering water. Let melt, stirring occasionally, then set aside to cool for about 5 minutes.

Put the butter and sugar in a large bowl and beat to combine, then beat in the egg yolks. Fold in the melted chocolate, then sift in the flour and cocoa powder and mix to combine. Stir in the milk, a little at a time, to loosen the mixture.

In a clean, grease-free bowl, whisk the egg whites until stiff, then fold into the chocolate mixture, about a quarter at a time. Spoon the cake mixture into the prepared tin and bake in the preheated oven for about 45 minutes, until a skewer inserted in the centre comes out clean. Remove from the oven and turn out on to a wire rack to cool completely.

To decorate, put the chocolate in a heatproof bowl, then put the cream in a saucepan and heat until almost boiling. Pour the hot cream over the chocolate and stir until melted. Leave to cool and thicken for about 10–15 minutes, then spread over the cake, smoothing it over the top and sides with a palette knife. Sprinkle with crystallized violets to decorate and let the frosting set before serving.

meringues with rosewater cream
Makes 8

Crispy, sugary meringues are a classic afternoon tea offering. Served as they are here – with a cream scented with delicately flavoured rosewater – they're truly sublime.

2 large egg whites
115 g caster sugar
2 baking trays, lined with baking parchment

FOR THE FILLING AND TO DECORATE
200 ml double cream
1½ tablespoons rosewater
a small handful of clean, fresh rose petals,
    to decorate (optional)

Preheat the oven to 130°C (250°F) Gas ½. Put the egg whites in a clean, grease-free bowl and whisk until they form stiff peaks. Whisk in the sugar, one tablespoonful at a time, until the mixture is thick and glossy.

Using two dessert spoons, shape about 16 meringues and place them on the baking trays. Bake for about 2 hours, until crisp and dry. Leave to cool on the baking trays, then carefully peel off the baking parchment.

To serve, whip the cream until it stands in soft peaks, then fold in the rosewater. Sandwich the meringues together with the cream and arrange on a serving plate. Scatter the rose petals, if using, over the meringues to decorate.

Bridal Shower

Nilgiri tea

champagne cocktails

savoury toasts

strawberry tartlets

creamy lemon cheesecake

A tea party makes an absolutely perfect gathering for a bridal shower. Make it a sophisticated and indulgent affair by serving sparkling champagne cocktails, elegant bite-sized savouries, delectable fresh fruit tartlets and a luxurious, melt-in-the-mouth cheesecake. The bride is the guest of honour and needs her friends to make her feel like a princess. Why not think of this party as a warm-up for the wedding day itself and pay extra special attention to all the details? Select beautiful table linens, glassware and china, and display the food on cake stands. It's a nice idea for each guest to bring a gift for the bride such as a piece of vintage jewellery, a handkerchief or a perfume bottle. These can be displayed as part of your décor to create an opulent and feminine atmosphere.

champagne cocktails
Serves 6

This classic champagne cocktail will bring sophistication and sparkle to any bridal shower.

6 white sugar cubes
Angostura Bitters, to taste
brandy, to taste
a bottle of chilled champagne
6 twists of lemon zest, to garnish
6 champagne flutes

Put a sugar cube in the bottom of each glass and add about 3 drops of Angostura Bitters to each. Add a splash of brandy (about 1 teaspoon is fine). Top up with chilled champagne and garnish with a twist of lemon. Serve immediately.

NILGIRI TEA
Some 1,500 miles south of Darjeeling and Assam, India's southern tea plantations stretch through the range of the Nilgiri Hills or 'Blue Mountains' that run down the south-western tip of the country. Most of Nilgiri's teas are used in blends, but more are now being marketed as single-source teas and are well worth trying. They produce a bright and fragrant brew with a delicate, slightly fruity flavour that makes them the perfect choice to complement this menu.

savoury toasts

Makes 24 (12 of each topping)

These tasty yet light, bite-sized toasts are perfect for whetting the appetite.

2 medium baguettes
olive oil for brushing

Preheat the grill to medium. Cut each baguette into about 12 thin slices. Lightly brush with oil, then toast on both sides until crisp and golden. Set aside to cool until needed.

FOR THE CHICKEN TOPPING

2 chicken breasts, cut into bite-sized strips
2 tablespoons olive oil, plus extra for brushing
1 garlic clove, crushed
2 tablespoons freshly squeezed lemon juice
6 tablespoons mayonnaise
3 teaspoons capers, finely chopped
a handful of fresh basil leaves, finely chopped, plus extra leaves to garnish
¼–½ teaspoon finely grated lemon zest
sea salt and freshly ground black pepper

FOR THE TUNA TOPPING

6 tablespoons crème fraîche
¼ teaspoon smoked paprika
¼ teaspoon ground cumin
½ garlic clove, crushed
½ teaspoon freshly grated lemon zest
½–1 teaspoon freshly squeezed lemon juice
100 g good-quality bottled tuna fillet in oil, drained
sea salt
fresh mint leaves, to garnish

To make the chargrilled chicken topping, arrange the chicken pieces in a shallow bowl. Put the oil, garlic and lemon juice in a small bowl and whisk to combine. Season with salt and pepper, then pour it over the chicken and toss to coat. Cover and chill. Put the mayonnaise, capers, chopped basil and lemon zest in a bowl and stir to combine. Season to taste with pepper. Set aside.

Brush a griddle pan with oil and set it over high heat. Add the chicken and cook for about 3 minutes, turning once, until cooked through. Meanwhile, spread 12 of the toasts with the mayonnaise mixture. Top with the chicken, and garnish with basil leaves to serve.

To make the tuna topping, combine the crème fraîche, paprika, cumin, garlic and lemon zest. Season to taste with lemon juice and add a little salt. Spoon the mixture on to the remaining toasts, top each one with a generous flake of tuna, and garnish with mint leaves to serve.

strawberry tartlets

Makes 12

These pretty little tartlets look impressive but are very easy to make. I cheat and use ready-made fresh custard for the filling so that the only cooking that's required is making the crisp almond pastry cases. Tiny wild strawberries are perfect, but if you can't find any, simply use slices of large strawberries.

3 tablespoons ground almonds
100 g plain flour
1 tablespoon caster sugar
50 g chilled butter, cubed
100 ml fresh ready-made custard
200 g strawberries
icing sugar, for dusting
a 12-hole mini tartlet tin, greased
a biscuit cutter, 6.5 cm in diameter

Put the ground almonds, flour and sugar in a food processor and pulse to combine. Add the butter and pulse again until the mixture resembles fine breadcrumbs. With the motor still running, gradually add 2 tablespoons water until the mixture comes together to form a dough. Wrap in clingfilm and chill for at least 30 minutes. Preheat the oven to 190°C (375°F) Gas 5. Roll out the pastry thinly and stamp out 12 rounds using a biscuit cutter. Press the rounds into the tartlet tin and prick the bases with a fork. Bake for about 12 minutes until crisp and golden. Remove from the oven, transfer to a wire rack and let cool.

To assemble, carefully spoon a little custard into the bottom of each tartlet case, top with a slice of strawberry and dust with a little icing sugar to serve.

A bridal shower will become a treasured memory for any bride-to-be, so pay attention to the details and make it a truly special occasion.

creamy lemon cheesecake
Serves 8–12

Nothing beats the satisfaction of a rich, creamy cheesecake, and this zesty one, with a gingery biscuit base, is just perfect. There's something about the fluffy white crème fraîche topping too that makes it look particularly bridal! It's delicious served as it is but, if you want to go the extra mile, serve decorated with generous curls of white chocolate or even fresh white rose petals.

150 g ginger nut biscuits
70 g butter, melted
400 g full-fat cream cheese
250 g mascarpone cheese
150 g caster sugar
grated zest and juice of 1 lemon
4 large eggs
a 20-cm springform cake tin, greased and tightly wrapped around the outside with a single sheet of foil
a medium roasting tin

FOR THE TOPPING AND DECORATION
200 ml crème fraîche or sour cream
1 tablespoon caster sugar
¼ teaspoon vanilla extract
white chocolate curls or rose petals (optional)

Put the biscuits in a plastic bag and crush them to fine crumbs using the end of a rolling pin. Add the crumbs to the melted butter and mix well to combine. Tip into the prepared tin, spread out evenly and then press down firmly with the underside of a glass to create a firm biscuit base. Chill for about 20 minutes.

Preheat the oven to 180°C (350°F) Gas 4. Beat together the cream cheese, mascarpone and sugar, then beat in the lemon zest and juice. Beat in the eggs one at a time. Spoon the mixture over the biscuit base and place the tin in a roasting tray. Pour boiling water around the tin to reach about halfway up the sides. Carefully place the roasting tray in the oven and bake for 45 minutes.

Beat together the crème fraîche, sugar and vanilla extract. Spoon the mixture over the top of the cheesecake in an even layer and return it to the oven for a further 15 minutes. Remove from the oven and let cool. Chill for at least 2 hours before serving. Decorate with white chocolate curls or rose petals.

Southern-style Tea

iced tea

topped cornbread toasts

chocolate pecan cookies

angel food cake

Give your guests a true taste of Southern-style hospitality. In the Southern states of America, iced tea is hugely popular and served poured from jugs into high-ball glasses or tumblers filled with ice, wedges of lemon and sprigs of fresh mint. This refreshing alternative to a hot cup of tea is the perfect libation to offer at a tea party on a swelteringly hot and humid summer afternoon. You may not be lucky enough to have a porch or verandah but take to the garden anyway. Throw a white lace cloth over the table and pile up plates of delicate savoury toasts, pecan cookies and a light-as-air angel food cake to welcome your friends.

iced tea
Makes 1 litre

5 heaped teaspoons black tea leaves
500 ml boiling water
500 ml cold water

TO SERVE
ice cubes
wedges of unwaxed lemon
mint leaves (optional)
white sugar, to taste

Put the tea leaves in a heatproof
jug or large teapot and pour in
the boiling water. Leave to
infuse for about 10 minutes to
get a really good, strong brew.
Strain into a jug and add the
cold water, leave to cool and
then chill. Serve poured over
ice with lemon wedges and mint
leaves, if using, and add sugar
to taste.

topped cornbread toasts
Makes 24

*Although cornbread is usually
served cut into chunks or
wedges, here it's toasted until
golden to give a nutty, crispy
base for fresh-tasting toppings.*

500 g cornbread

FOR THE CRAB SALAD TOPPING
170-g tin white crabmeat
½ green pepper, deseeded and diced
1 teaspoon freshly squeezed
   lemon juice
2 teaspoons olive oil
a good splash of Tabasco sauce
½ garlic clove, finely chopped
1 teaspoon snipped chives

FOR THE AVOCADO SALSA TOPPING
1 ripe avocado, stoned, peeled
   and finely diced
2 tomatoes, deseeded and finely
   diced
2 spring onions, sliced
1 red chilli, deseeded and finely
   chopped
a handful fresh coriander, chopped
½ lime
sea salt

To make the crab salad, put
the crabmeat and green pepper
in a bowl. Put the lemon juice,
olive oil, Tabasco and garlic
in a small bowl and whisk to
combine. Pour it over the crab
and pepper mixture. Sprinkle
with chives and toss well to
combine. Cover and set aside.

To make the avocado salsa,
put the avocado, tomato,
spring onion and chilli in a bowl.
Sprinkle with the coriander and
add a pinch of salt, if liked, then
squeeze the lime juice over it
and toss gently to combine.
Cover and set aside.

Preheat the grill. Slice the
cornbread into 24 squares
measuring about 5 cm x 5 cm
and 1 cm thick. Arrange the
slices under the hot grill and
toast on both sides until golden
brown and crisp.

To assemble, put spoonfuls
of crab salad on to half of the
toasts and avocado salsa
on the remainder. Serve them
immediately, as the toasts will
lose their crispness if left too
long before eating.

ICED TEA

Iced tea was invented at
the 1904 World's Fair in
St Louis, when a merchant
of Indian tea was faced with
the challenge of selling hot
tea to crowds sweltering
in the summer heat. In
desperation, he poured his
tea over ice and the cool,
copper-coloured beverage
was an instant sensation.
Every true Southern belle
has her own special way of
making the perfect pitcher
and the recipe here is just
one way. Let your guests
sweeten their tea to taste.

chocolate pecan cookies
Makes about 14

Pecans are grown widely across the Southern states, so big, buttery and crumbly pecan cookies are the obvious choice for this Southern-style tea party. And of course, no cookie is really complete without a generous amount of chunky chocolate chips.

175 g butter, at room temperature
100 g caster sugar
1 tablespoon full-fat milk
200 g self-raising flour
100 g plain chocolate, roughly chopped
50 g pecan nuts, roughly chopped
14 pecan halves, to decorate
2–3 baking trays, greased

Preheat the oven to 180°C (350°F) Gas 4.

Put the butter and sugar in a bowl and beat together until smooth and creamy, then beat in the milk. Add the flour and mix to make a soft dough, then add the chocolate and chopped pecan nuts.

Drop 14 rounded tablespoonfuls of the mixture on to the baking trays (spacing them well apart to allow the mixture to spread), and flatten them slightly with the back of the spoon. Press a pecan half into the centre of each one.

Bake for about 15 minutes, until golden around the edges, then leave to cool on the trays for about 5 minutes before transferring to a wire rack to cool completely.

These cookies are best eaten on the day they are baked, but will keep for a few days in an airtight container.

The British may be experts at making and serving a traditional cup of hot tea, but when it comes to iced tea, the Americans definitely have the edge.

angel food cake

Serves 8–12

This pure white, whisked sponge cake is the classic all-American cake. It's traditionally baked in a ring-shaped tin and tastes divine served with blueberries or juicy wedges of ripe peach.

125 g plain flour
250 g caster sugar
10 egg whites
1 teaspoon cream of tartar
½ teaspoon vanilla extract
a punnet of blueberries or 6 ripe peaches, to serve (optional)
a 25-cm diameter ring mould or a non-stick angel cake tin, lightly greased

FOR THE FROSTING
115 g caster sugar
2 egg whites
2 teaspoons golden syrup
½ teaspoon vanilla extract

Preheat the oven to 180°C (350°F) Gas 4. In a large bowl, sift together the flour and half the sugar three times, until very light. Set aside.

In a separate, grease-free bowl, whisk the egg whites with the cream of tartar until stiff, then gradually whisk in the remaining sugar until the mixture is thick and glossy. Whisk in the vanilla extract.

Sift half the flour and sugar mixture into the egg whites and gently fold in, then sift in the remaining flour and fold in.

Spoon the cake mixture into the prepared mould and bake for about 40 minutes, until a skewer inserted into the cake comes out clean. Turn the cake out on to a wire rack and leave to cool completely before frosting.

To make the frosting, put the sugar in a small saucepan with 4 tablespoons water and heat, stirring until the sugar dissolves, then boil until the temperature reaches 240°F.

In a clean, grease-free bowl, whisk the egg whites until very stiff, then gradually pour the sugar syrup into the egg whites in a thin stream, whisking constantly until thick and glossy. Whisk in the golden syrup and vanilla extract and continue whisking until the frosting has cooled. Use a palette knife to spread it over the cooled cake. Serve with blueberries or slices of fresh peach, as preferred.

Russian Tea Ceremony

Russian caravan tea

iced lemon vodka

blinis with sour cream
and caviar

hazelnut tea cookies

Russian poppy seed cake

Tea was first introduced to Russia from China in the seventeeth

century and is now hugely popular throughout Russian society.

Central to the Russian tea ceremony is the samovar – an ornate

device that is part-urn and part-teapot. The lower unit is an urn with

a tap in which water is boiled, while on top a teapot rests in which

a tea is brewed. This strong, black infusion is then poured and

diluted according to taste with water from the urn below. The tea is

often served in glasses with ornate metal holders. If you want to host

a truly authentic Russian tea ceremony a samovar is a must – they

can be hired relatively easily. No Russian party would be complete

without vodka, so I've included a lemon-infused one here.

iced lemon vodka
Serves 8

The Russians are renowned for enjoying vodka, their national tipple, at any time of day. The sharp, intensely refreshing flavour goes particularly well with blinis and strong black tea.

freshly squeezed juice of 2 lemons
   plus slices of lemon to serve
175 g sugar
125 ml vodka
a resealable bottle or container
8 freezer-frosted shot glasses

Put the lemon juice in a jug, add the sugar and stir until it has dissolved. Add the vodka, transfer the liquid to the bottle and chill in the freezer. Serve in freezer-frosted shot glasses with small slices of lemon to garnish.

RUSSIAN CARAVAN TEA
This is a blend of black teas from China which has a slightly smoky flavour. It recreates the taste of the teas that were transported back to Moscow from the Chinese border after furs had been traded for tea. Since the journey by camel caravan was long and slow, the traders had to camp. They would stop for the night and light fires to keep warm and cook food. It's believed that the tea absorbed a little smoke from the fires. Today, Russian caravan blends often include a hint of lapsang souchong to achieve a similar effect.

Over the last 200 years, the tea ceremony has become one of the most pervasive cultural traditions in Central Russia.

blinis with sour cream and caviar
Makes about 30

Traditional Russian blinis are made with a yeasted batter, but these are leavened with baking powder and are much quicker to make. They provide the perfect base for the sour cream and salty caviar, which explodes tantalizingly on your tongue. If you are short of time, you can buy ready-made blinis to warm up in the oven.

80 g plain flour
70 g buckwheat flour
1 teaspoon baking powder
a good pinch of sea salt
1 egg
200 ml milk
25 g butter, melted, plus extra
   for greasing

FOR THE TOPPING
80 ml sour cream or crème fraîche
½ teaspoon finely grated lemon zest
2–3 tablespoons caviar, salmon roe
   (or roughly chopped smoked
   salmon, if preferred)
freshly ground black pepper

Put the sour cream in a bowl and add the lemon zest. Stir to combine, then cover and store in the fridge until needed.

Set a griddle or frying pan over low heat. Combine the flours, baking powder and salt in a bowl and make a well in the centre. Beat together the egg, milk and melted butter, then pour into the well. Gradually work in the flour, using a fork to make a smooth batter.

Lightly grease a frying pan or griddle with butter, using a piece of kitchen paper. Drop small spoonfuls of the blini batter into the pan. Cook for about 2 minutes, until bubbles appear on the surface, then flip over and cook for a further minute, or until golden. As you make the blinis, keep them warm in a low oven.

To serve, top each blini with a little sour cream and about ¼ teaspoon of caviar. Grind a little black pepper on top and serve immediately.

hazelnut tea cookies
Makes 12

Frequently referred to as Russian teacakes, these plump, round, sugared cookies look wonderful piled up on a little plate alongside the ubiquitous poppy seed cake. These are made with hazelnuts, but popular variations are made with almonds and walnuts.

75 g butter, at room temperature
25 g icing sugar, sifted, plus extra for rolling
¼ teaspoon vanilla extract
40 g toasted hazelnuts, finely chopped
100 g plain flour

Preheat the oven to 180°C (350°F) Gas 4. Put the butter and icing sugar in a bowl and beat until smooth. Add the vanilla extract and hazelnuts and mix to combine. Add the flour and bring the mixture together to make a stiff dough.

With cool hands, roll the dough into 12 balls – each about 3 cm in diameter – and arrange them on a greased baking tray. Bake for about 12 minutes, until a pale golden colour.

Spoon about 4 heaped tablespoons of icing sugar into a wide, shallow bowl. While the cookies are still hot from the oven, roll them in the sugar to coat, then transfer to a wire rack to cool. When completely cool, roll in sugar a second time to coat. (Add more icing sugar to the bowl if necessary.)

Russian poppy seed cake
Serves 8–12

You will find versions of this classic cake all over Russia, the Ukraine and Eastern Europe. It is delicious eaten with the strong, dark tea favoured by Russians. The poppy seeds give it a subtle yet distinctive flavour and striking dark appearance when you cut into it.

115 g poppy seeds
160 ml milk
125 g butter, at room temperature
250 g caster sugar
1 teaspoon vanilla extract
2 eggs, separated
200 g plain flour
2 teaspoons baking powder
¼ teaspoon sea salt
icing sugar, for dusting
a 2-lb capacity loaf tin, greased and lined with greaseproof paper

Put the poppy seeds in a food processor or blender and process for about 1 minute, until finely chopped and almost damp-looking in appearance. Tip the seeds into a saucepan, pour in the milk and bring to the boil, stirring once or twice. Remove from the heat and leave to sit for about 1 hour.

Preheat the oven to 180°C (350°F) Gas 4.

Put the butter and sugar in a bowl and beat until smooth and creamy. Beat in the vanilla extract and egg yolks. Add the poppy seed and milk mixture and mix well until thoroughly combined.

Combine the flour, baking powder and salt. Sift it into the poppy seed mixture and fold in. Put the egg whites in a separate, grease-free bowl and whisk until stiff, then fold into the cake mixture a few tablespoonfuls at a time. Tip the mixture into the prepared loaf tin and level the surface. Bake for about 1 hour, or until a skewer inserted in the centre of the cake comes out clean. Remove from the oven, then lift the cake out of the tin and leave to cool on a wire rack. Dust liberally with icing sugar to serve.

Gentleman's Tea

Yunnan tea

boiled eggs
with asparagus 'dippers'

smoked mackerel pâté
on toast

drop scones
with cinnamon butter

rich fruit cake

This classic tea has a definite air of masculine sophistication about it. Inspired by the unique environment of a traditional gentlemen's club, the menu would be right at home served amidst rustling newspapers and wing-backed leather armchairs. The food is designed to appeal to men's appetites, so it's generous on the savouries, with simple drop scones and a rich, old-fashioned fruit cake to follow. Make this wonderful tea as a special treat for any man in your life – husband, father, grandfather, brother or son – and create the opportunity for him to escape the stresses and strains of daily life and while away a leisurely hour or two over a pot of tea.

boiled eggs with asparagus 'dippers'
Serves 2

Although perhaps a slightly unusual choice for an afternoon tea party, soft-boiled eggs are a good accompaniment for the crisp toasts spread with smoked mackerel pâté. Tender asparagus spears are a luxury alternative to 'soldiers' and perfect for dipping into runny, golden yolks.

2 eggs
150 g fresh asparagus, trimmed
sea salt and freshly ground black
   pepper

Place the eggs in a saucepan of water and simmer for 3–4 minutes only. Drain and place in egg cups.

Meanwhile, fill a frying pan with salted boiling water to a depth of about 3 cm. Add the asparagus and blanch for about 3 minutes, until just tender. Drain well and pat dry on kitchen paper.

To serve, carefully slice the tops off the eggs. Serve with the asparagus spears on the side for dipping into the runny yolks and provide little dishes of salt and black pepper to season.

YUNNAN TEA

For a robust menu full of savoury and salty flavours such as this one, you need a sturdy tea that can can hold its own. The Yunnan province of China has been producing tea for 1,700 years, and any blend from this region would be a good choice. The tea produces a rich, dark, reddish-black brew with a molasses-like sweetness and malty flavour that's best enjoyed with a little milk.

smoked mackerel pâté on toast
Serves 4

Similar in style to the famous anchovy butter, Gentleman's Relish, this is the ideal way to start this substantial tea. The pâté can be stored in the fridge for up to three days.

200 g smoked mackerel fillets, skinned
120 g mascarpone cheese
a pinch of freshly grated nutmeg
freshly squeezed juice of ½ lemon
freshly ground black pepper
thin slices of toasted granary bread, to serve

Put the mackerel fillets in a bowl and use a fork to flake them. Transfer to a food processor and add the mascarpone, nutmeg, a little lemon juice and a good grinding of pepper. Blend to make a smooth pâté, then stir in more lemon juice to taste.

Spoon the pâté into four small ramekins, or a single serving dish, and serve with plenty of hot granary toast.

drop scones with cinnamon butter
Makes about 20

Cinnamon butter is delicious spread on warm drop scones, straight from the pan. This recipe makes about twice as much butter as you need, so you can keep the rest in the fridge to enjoy another time.

115 g self-raising flour
1 tablespoon caster sugar
1 egg, beaten
150 ml full-fat milk
vegetable oil, for brushing

FOR THE CINNAMON BUTTER
85 g butter, at room temperature
4 teaspoons icing sugar
½ teaspoon ground cinnamon

To make the cinnamon butter, beat together the butter, icing sugar and cinnamon until smooth and creamy. Either spoon the butter into a small dish and level the top, or wrap it in clingfilm and shape into a log that can be chilled until firm and sliced into rounds to serve.

To make the drop scones, put the flour and sugar in a bowl and mix to combine. Make a well in the centre. Add the egg and half the milk, and gradually work in the flour to make a smooth batter. Beat in the remaining milk.

Set a large, non-stick frying pan over low heat. Brush the hot pan with oil, then wipe off any excess using kitchen paper. Drop tablespoonfuls of batter into the pan and cook for 1–2 minutes, until bubbles appear on the surface. Flip over each drop scone and cook for a further 30 seconds–1 minute until golden. Keep the cooked scones warm as you go.

Serve warm with generous pats of the cinnamon butter for spreading.

rich fruit cake
Serves 8–12

This cake improves with keeping so if you can, make it several days beforehand.

175 g butter
100 g caster sugar
50 g soft brown sugar
3 eggs
grated zest of 1 unwaxed orange
200 g self-raising flour
1 teaspoon baking powder
2 tablespoons brandy
200 g mixed dried vine fruits
50 g dried figs, chopped
100 g dried apricots, chopped
50 g glacé cherries, halved
50 g blanched almonds
an 18-cm cake tin, lined with greaseproof paper

Preheat the oven to 160°C (325°F) Gas 3. Put the butter and sugar in a bowl and beat until fluffy. Beat in the eggs one at a time. Stir in the orange zest, then sift in the flour and baking powder. Mix well to combine. Stir in the brandy, followed by the fruit.

Tip the mixture into the prepared tin and spread it out evenly. Arrange the almonds on top in concentric circles. Bake for about 1 hour 10 minutes, until a dark, golden colour and a skewer inserted in the centre comes out clean. Leave to cool in the tin for about 20 minutes, then turn out on to a wire rack to cool completely. Wrap in foil, and store in an airtight container until ready to slice and serve.

High Tea

Assam tea

smoked trout rarebit

almond biscotti

orange tuiles

coffee and walnut cake

High tea is an old-fashioned tradition. Unlike other afternoon teas, which are served between lunch and the evening meal, high tea is considered much more of a meal in itself. It is often served slightly later than traditional afternoon tea – perhaps at five o'clock or so – and provides an early evening supper with a more substantial savoury (often served hot) than a classic teatime menu. This is, of course, still followed by the usual teatime fancies and a large, indulgent cake. High tea is perfect enjoyed as a pre-theatre supper, when there isn't time for dinner before curtain-up.

smoked trout rarebit
Serves 4

A luxury version of cheese on toast, these hearty rarebits are the ideal high tea savoury. Wonderfully comforting, with an oozing, melted topping, they provide just the right combination of indulgence and sustenance.

2 smoked trout fillets, skinned and flaked
4 thick slices of wholegrain bread
175 g Cheddar or Gruyère, grated
3½ tablespoons dry white wine
¼ small onion, finely chopped
freshly ground black pepper
chopped fresh parsley, to serve

Preheat the grill. Grill the bread on one side until golden.

Meanwhile, put the cheese and wine in a saucepan and set over low heat. Gently heat, stirring constantly, until melted.

When the bread is golden on one side, turn the slices over and arrange a quarter of the smoked trout on each. Spoon some melted cheese mixture over the top and scatter with some chopped onion. Season with a little black pepper and return to the grill until golden and bubbling. Sprinkle with a little parsley and serve immediately.

ASSAM TEA
Assam, 'the land of the one-horned rhino', is a vast and beautiful area of India, through which the mighty Brahmaputra river runs, carrying rich, fertile soil with it. Assam is the largest tea-growing region in the world, producing 425,000 tonnes per year. Teas grown here are a distinctive brown colour with gold flecks and produce a rich, malty and exquisitely smooth brew that's best drunk with milk.

almond biscotti

Makes about 20

These crunchy finger biscuits which snap so enticingly between your teeth, offer a lighter alternative to the other sweet treats on the table at high tea – they are not too sweet, and delightfully nutty.

85 g plain flour
85 g self-raising flour
60 g polenta
85 g caster sugar
2 eggs
1 teaspoon vanilla extract
85 g blanched almonds

Preheat the oven to 160°C (325°F) Gas 3. Sift the flours, polenta and sugar into a large bowl and make a well in the centre. Lightly beat the eggs and vanilla extract, then pour into the dry ingredients. Add the almonds and stir together, then knead gently to form a sticky dough.

Use your hands to shape the dough into a flat log about 20 cm x 10 cm x 2 cm and place it on a greased baking tray. Bake for about 30 minutes, until golden.

Remove from the oven and let cool for about 5 minutes, then transfer to a chopping board. Using a serrated knife, gently slice the log into slices 7 mm thick and arrange them on the baking tray. Return to the oven and bake for a further 15–20 minutes, until crisp and golden.

Remove from the oven and transfer to a wire rack to cool.

This satisfying tea makes a great choice for a birthday celebration, when a surprise trip to the theatre is planned for the evening.

orange tuiles
Makes 14

Delicate, melt-in-the-mouth tuiles with their elegant rounded shape are a welcome addition to this menu. Their daintiness makes them perfect if your guests only want a little sweet something to follow the rarebit.

1 egg white
50 g caster sugar
freshly grated zest of 1 unwaxed
    orange
25 g butter, melted and cooled
25 g plain flour
*2 baking trays, lined with
    greaseproof paper and lightly
    greased*

Preheat the oven to 190°C (375°F) Gas 5.

Put the egg white in a large, grease-free bowl and whisk to form stiff peaks. Sprinkle with the sugar and orange zest and fold in. Add half the butter, sift in half the flour and fold in. Repeat with the remaining butter and flour.

Working in batches, drop 4 teaspoonfuls of the mixture on to one of the prepared baking trays, spacing them well apart. Spread out into thin rounds using the back of the teaspoon. Repeat with the rest of the mixture. Bake for about 5–6 minutes, until a pale golden colour. Leave to cool for just a few seconds, then carefully remove from the tray using a spatula, and drape over a rolling pin to cool. They will take on a curved shape as they crisp up. Transfer to a wire rack to cool completely.

coffee and walnut cake
Serves 8–12

This classic teatime cake is enduringly popular, perhaps because something magical happens when coffee and walnuts come together.

180 g butter, at room temperature
180 g caster sugar
3 eggs
180 g self-raising flour
2 teaspoons instant coffee granules,
    dissolved in 1 tablespoon
    hot water

60 g walnut pieces
*2 x 20-cm diameter sandwich tins,
    greased and base-lined*

FOR THE FROSTING
250 g mascarpone cheese
85 g icing sugar, sifted
1½ teaspoons instant coffee granules,
    dissolved in 1½ teaspoons
    hot water
walnut halves, to decorate

Preheat the oven to 180°C (350°F) Gas 4.

Put the butter and sugar in a large bowl and cream together until pale and fluffy. Beat in the eggs one at a time. Sift the flour into the butter mixture and stir to combine. Fold in the walnuts and coffee. Divide the cake mixture between the two prepared tins and level out the surface of each.

Bake for 20–25 minutes until golden and the sponge springs back when gently pressed or a skewer inserted in the centre comes out clean. Transfer to a wire rack, carefully peel off the paper and let cool completely before frosting.

To make the frosting, beat together the mascarpone, icing sugar and coffee until smooth and creamy. Spread slightly less than half of the frosting over one of the cooled cakes, then place the second cake on top. Spread the remaining frosting over the top and decorate with walnut halves to finish.

Fireside Tea

lapsang souchong tea

warm Parmesan and bacon
pancakes with chive butter

toasted teacakes

sticky marzipan and
cherry loaf

stem ginger biscuits

Enjoy this cosy, homely tea in autumn and winter when the

temperatures drop and the nights are drawing in earlier each day.

Why not enjoy a bracing afternoon walk in the crisp air to build

up an appetite, then return home to light a fire in the grate, pull up

armchairs around the fire and snuggle down for tea. The menu,

from the pot of smoky, aromatic tea to the savoury pancakes,

toasted teacakes, spicy ginger biscuits and a sticky loaf cake,

provides a truly nostalgic and comforting tea, guaranteed to ward

off the winter blues and bring a warm glow to your guests' cheeks.

LAPSANG SOUCHONG TEA

The distinctive, smoky flavour of this large-leafed black China tea makes it a good choice for a fireside tea – with its delicious, almost tarry fragrance reflecting the warm glow and crackle of logs in the grate. The enticing aroma of the tea is achieved by drying the leaves over pinewood fires, and the best leaves are said to come from the hills in northern Fujian. Lapsang souchong has a golden colour when brewed and may be drunk black or with a little milk.

warm parmesan and bacon pancakes with chive butter

Makes about 20

Served warm from the pan, the combination of smoky bacon pancakes and chive butter is a lovely winter treat and a good way to start this fireside tea.

1 tablespoon vegetable oil, plus extra
　for brushing
3 strips of bacon, snipped into small
　pieces, or 75 g pancetta, cubed
115 g self-raising flour
25 g Parmesan cheese, grated
a pinch of sea salt
1 egg, beaten
150 ml full-fat milk
freshly ground black pepper

FOR THE CHIVE BUTTER
85 g butter, at room temperature
2–2½ tablespoons snipped chives
freshly ground black pepper

To make the chive butter, put the butter in a bowl and beat in the chives. Season with black pepper. Spoon the mixture into a ramekin or small serving bowl, cover and chill until needed.

Heat the oil a large, non-stick frying pan and fry the bacon for about 3 minutes, until crispy. Remove from the pan and drain off any grease. Wipe the pan with kitchen paper and leave set over low heat.

Put the flour, cheese and salt in a large bowl and season well with pepper. Make a well in the middle. Add the egg and half the milk and gradually work in the flour to make a smooth batter. Beat in the remaining milk to make a smooth batter.

Drop tablespoonfuls of batter into the pan, sprinkle a little bacon on top and cook for 1–2 minutes, until bubbles appear on the surface. Flip over the pancake and cook for a further 30 seconds–1 minute, until a golden colour. Keep warm while you cook the remaining mixture. Serve with the chive butter.

toasted teacakes

Makes 8

There's something particularly comforting and homely about a plateful of freshly toasted teacakes dripping with butter, and the wonderful smell of spices that they always emit. If you've got an old-fashioned toasting fork with a long handle, why not toast the teacakes the traditional way over the open fire.

225 g strong white bread flour
½ teaspoon sea salt
1 teaspoon easy-blend dried yeast
15 g soft brown sugar
¼ teaspoon freshly grated nutmeg
60 g mixed dried vine fruits
40 g butter, melted

120 ml full-fat milk, plus extra
  for brushing
butter, to serve

Sift the flour, salt, yeast, sugar and nutmeg into a large bowl. Stir in the dried fruits and make a well in the centre.

Put the milk and butter in a small saucepan and heat together until just warm. Pour into the flour mixture and gradually work together to make a soft dough. Turn out on to a lightly floured work surface and knead for about 5 minutes, until smooth and elastic. Place in a bowl, slip the bowl into a large plastic bag, seal with a rubber band and leave to rise for 1 hour, until doubled in size.

When risen, tip the dough out on to a lightly floured work surface, punch down, and divide into eight pieces of equal size. Shape each one into a ball, flatten slightly and arrange on a greased baking tray, spacing slightly apart. Slip the tray into a large plastic bag and leave the dough to rise again for 45 minutes, until doubled in size.

Preheat the oven to 200°C (400°F) Gas 6. Brush the top of each teacake with milk, then bake for about 15 minutes, until risen and golden and sounds hollow when the base is gently tapped. Transfer to a wire rack to cool. When ready to serve, split, toast on the cut sides and spread generously with butter.

sticky marzipan and cherry loaf

Serves 8–12

Studded with sweet glacé cherries and with a surprise layer of sticky marzipan running through the centre, this simple loaf cake will hit the spot.

175 g butter, at room temperature
175 g caster sugar
3 eggs
175 g self-raising flour
85 g ground almonds
175 g glacé cherries, halved
75 g chilled marzipan, finely grated
icing sugar, for dusting
a 2-lb loaf tin, greased and lined

Preheat the oven to 180°C (350°F) Gas 4. Put the butter and sugar in a large bowl and beat until pale and creamy. Beat in the eggs one at a time. Sift in the flour and fold in, then stir in the cherries until evenly distributed in the mixture. Spoon half the mixture into the prepared loaf tin and level the surface. Sprinkle with the grated marzipan. Top with the remaining mixture and smooth the surface.

Bake for about 45 minutes, then remove the cake from the oven and cover the top with foil. Return it to the oven and bake for a further 25 minutes, until risen and golden and a skewer inserted in the centre of the cake comes out clean. Leave the cake to cool in the tin for about 10 minutes, then lift out on to a wire rack to cool. Serve the cake slightly warm or at room temperature.

stem ginger biscuits

Makes about 10

The spicy and chewy pieces of stem ginger give a kick to these buttery, melt-in-the-mouth biscuits which are delicious with a pot of warming lapsang souchong tea. They are the perfect addition to this cosy fireside tea.

85 g butter, at room temperature
75 g golden caster sugar
1 egg yolk
½ teaspoon ground ginger
60 g stem ginger in syrup (about 3 balls), chopped
25 g ground almonds
115 g self-raising flour
2 baking trays, lined with baking parchment

Preheat the oven to 160°C (325°F) Gas 3. Beat the butter and sugar together until pale and creamy, then beat in the egg yolk. Stir in the ground ginger and stem ginger, then the ground almonds. Add the flour and mix well.

Roll the mixture into about ten walnut-sized balls and arrange them on the prepared baking trays, spacing well apart. Flatten slightly with your fingers and bake for about 20 minutes, until a pale golden brown colour.

Leave the biscuits to cool on the baking trays for a few minutes, until slightly firm, then use a spatula to transfer them to a wire rack to cool.

Moroccan Tea

mint tea

toasted flatbreads
with quail's eggs and
toasted cumin seeds

scented butter biscuits

gazelle's horns

yoghurt and pistachio cake

Hospitality is of the highest importance in Morocco. Even in the humblest of homes, a visitor will always be offered a steaming glass of refreshing mint tea, perhaps with some sweetmeats or fruit. The art of making tea is steeped in ritual, with a great deal of ceremony in brewing and pouring. The sugar is chipped off a large, cone-shaped block and added straight to the teapot – usually a decorative silver one – and the tea is poured into small, ornate glasses edged with gold. On festive occasions, two teapots, one for each hand, will be held high above the glasses to create a thick froth on top. Why not extend some Moroccan-style hospitality to your friends and invite them to join you for this sensual feast?

mint tea
Serves 4

4 teaspoons Chinese gunpowder tea
    or other green tea
a large handful of fresh mint leaves
sugar, to taste

Pour a little boiling water into
a teapot to warm the pot, then
tip the water away. Add the
tea and mint and fill the pot with
boiling water. Leave to infuse for
about 5 minutes, then sweeten
to taste with sugar. Pour into
tea glasses to serve.

MOROCCAN MINT TEA
In Morocco, tea is always flavoured with fresh mint leaves
and served extremely sweet. Although the making and
offering of tea is now regarded as an institution, it only
arrived in North Africa in 1854 during the Crimean War,
when British tea merchants were hindered by the blockade in
the Baltic and had to seek new markets, such as Tangier, for
their imported China tea. Nowadays, the ubiquitous sweet
and refreshing mint tea of Morocco is the national drink.

toasted flatbreads with quail's eggs and toasted cumin seeds
Makes 12

In Morocco, tiny quail's eggs dipped in toasted cumin seeds and salt are served as a traditional snack or 'kemia'. I've adapted this idea to create an bite-sized teatime savoury by serving them on warm, garlicky pitta bread with a hint of chilli.

12 quail's eggs
1½ teaspoons cumin seeds
2 tablespoons olive oil
2 garlic cloves, finely chopped
3 pitta bread
a pinch of crushed dried chilli flakes
chopped flat-leaf parsley, to serve
sea salt flakes

Put the eggs in a saucepan filled with boiling water and cook for 3–4 minutes. Drain and leave to cool. Carefully peel and halve.

Meanwhile, toast the cumin seeds in a dry frying pan for about 1 minute, until they give off their aroma. Roughly grind in a pestle and mortar and set aside. Heat the oil in a frying pan and add the garlic. Fry for just 30 seconds. Remove the oil from the heat and set aside.

Preheat the grill. Toast the pitta breads on both sides, then slice each one into four fingers. Drizzle the garlicky oil over each one, then top with a halved quail's egg. Sprinkle with plenty of toasted cumin seeds, a little chilli, a pinch of salt flakes and fresh parsley to serve.

When in season, orange blossom is added to mint tea to give it a refreshing floral lift. In winter, herbs such as sage and thyme, or dried rose and geranium petals might be used.

scented butter biscuits
Makes about 16

You will find many variations of these little almond-topped butter biscuits all over Morocco. They are often flavoured with orange flower water or delicately scented with cinnamon, as here.

150 g butter, at room temperature
75 g icing sugar
½ teaspoon ground cinnamon
200 g plain flour
16 blanched almonds
2 baking trays, greased

Preheat the oven to 180°C (350°F) Gas 4. Put the butter, sugar and cinnamon in a bowl and beat until smooth and creamy. Sift in the flour, mix to combine and bring together until the mixture forms a soft dough.

Break off walnut-sized pieces of the dough and roll into balls. Press the balls gently between the palms of your hands to flatten slightly. Arrange the biscuits on the baking trays and press an almond on top of each one to decorate.

Bake for about 17 minutes, until the biscuits are a pale golden colour. Let cool on the baking trays for a couple of minutes before transferring to a wire rack to cool completely.

gazelle's horns
Makes 12

These poetically named pastries, filled with almond paste, are a Moroccan speciality and often served mid-afternoon with a glass of mint tea. They are flavoured with orange flower water, which you can find in most large supermarkets.

FOR THE PASTRY
250 g plain flour
1 egg yolk
60 ml sunflower oil
5–6 tablespoons cold water
a biscuit cutter, 8.5 cm in diameter

FOR THE FILLING
150 g ground almonds
75 g icing sugar, plus extra
   for dusting
25 g butter, at room temperature
1 tablespoon orange flower water,
   plus extra for sprinkling

To make the pastry, sift the flour into a large bowl, then add the egg yolk and oil and roughly stir in. Using your fingers, work the ingredients together until thoroughly combined and the mixture is the texture of damp sand. Add sufficient water to make a soft dough. Turn the dough out on to a floured work surface and knead until smooth and pliable. Wrap in clingfilm then let rest for 30 minutes.

Preheat the oven to 200°C (400°F) Gas 6.

To make the filling, put the almonds and sugar in a food processor and process until very finely ground and starting to stick together. Add the butter and orange flower water and blend into a soft paste.

Divide the almond paste into 12 balls of equal size, then roll each ball into a finger about 6.5 cm long, with tapering ends.

Using a rolling pin, roll the chilled dough to a thickness of about 1.5 cm. Use a biscuit cutter to stamp out 12 rounds. Place a finger of almond paste in the centre of each round and fold the pastry over the top, pressing the dough around the edge to seal. Bend each pastry semi-circle slightly to create a crescent moon shape.

Arrange the crescents on a baking tray and prick each one with a fork. Bake for about 12–15 minutes, until barely coloured. Remove from the oven and transfer to a wire rack to cool.

Sprinkle or brush each one with a little orange flower water and dust liberally with icing sugar to serve.

yoghurt and pistachio cake
Serves 8

This light, fluffy cake with a texture similar to cheesecake, is best served cold or chilled.

3 eggs, separated
85 g caster sugar
60 ml sour cream
1½ tablespoons plain flour
250 g Greek yoghurt
grated zest and freshly squeezed
   juice of 1 unwaxed lemon
1–2 drops vanilla extract, to taste
25 g pistachio nuts, chopped
a medium ovenproof baking dish
a large roasting tray

Put the egg yolks and 60 g of the sugar in a large bowl and whisk for a couple of minutes until thick and pale. In a separate bowl, stir together the sour cream and flour until well mixed, then fold in the yoghurt, lemon zest and juice, and vanilla extract to taste. Stir this mixture into the whisked egg yolks.

In a separate, large, grease-free bowl, whisk the egg whites until they form stiff peaks, then sprinkle in the remaining sugar and whisk until very stiff and glossy. Add the yoghurt and egg yolk mixture and gently fold together. Pour or spoon the mixture into a baking dish.

Place the dish in a roasting tray. Pour in sufficient cold water to reach about halfway up the sides of the dish, then bake for 20 minutes. Carefully slide the dish out of the oven, sprinkle the cake with the nuts and return it to the oven to bake for a further 15–20 minutes, until a golden colour and firm to the touch.

Remove the cake from the oven and let cool. Chill in the fridge until ready to serve. This cake is best eaten fresh.

Tropical Tea

tropical tea punch

spicy chicken satay sticks

tropical fruit skewers

wafer-thin spice biscuits

pineapple cake with
lime syrup

Bring a taste of the tropics into your home by throwing this zany

tropical tea party. With jewel-bright colours, exotic fruits, fragrant

spices and fiery flavours to set your taste buds tingling, the menu

will help to transport you to another land. Whether you decide to

throw a garden tea party in the blazing sunshine of summer or bring

a little cheer to a dreary winter's day, this tantalizing flavours on offer

are sure to bring out the feel-good factor in all your guests. To get

the party off to a sizzling start, why not present everyone with a

Hawaiian lei (floral garland) as they arrive?

TROPICAL TEA PUNCH

A large jug or bowl of fruity tea punch is a fun accompaniment to the food at this colourful tea party. This refreshing blend of black leaf tea, pineapple juice and rum, garnished with slices of exotic and citrus fruit, would be perfect served in the hazy heat of a tropical afternoon. If you want to make this punch for children, use decaffeinated tea and leave out the rum.

tropical tea punch
Makes about 1¼ litres

3 teaspoons black tea leaves, such
  as Keemun or Nilgiri
1–2 tablespoons soft brown sugar,
  to taste
600 ml unsweetened pineapple juice,
  well chilled
4 tablespoons white rum
1 lime, sliced
1 orange, sliced
1 star fruit, thinly sliced
ice cubes, to serve

Pour a little hot water into a large teapot and leave to warm for a minute or two. Drain, add the tea leaves and pour in the freshly boiled water. Leave the tea to brew for about 3 minutes.

Strain the tea into a large glass jug and add sugar to taste. When it has cooled, add the pineapple juice and rum. Chill in the fridge. To serve, add the fruit slices and plenty of ice to the jug and pour into tumblers.

spicy chicken satay sticks
Makes 12

These classic South-East Asian bites, dipped in a spicy peanut sauce, make a fabulous savoury for serving at this tropical tea party. You can marinate the chicken skewers in advance, then simply pop them under the grill to cook when your guests arrive.

3 skinless chicken breasts
1 garlic clove, crushed
1 teaspoon grated fresh root ginger
a pinch of crushed dried chilli flakes
freshly squeezed juice of 1 lime
1 teaspoon Thai fish sauce
*12 bamboo or wooden skewers,
  soaked in cold water*

FOR THE PEANUT SAUCE
4 tablespoons coconut milk
5 tablespoons crunchy peanut butter
½ garlic clove, crushed
1 green chilli, deseeded and finely
  chopped
freshly squeezed juice of ½–1 lime
soy sauce, to taste

Slice each chicken breast into four long strips and put in a shallow dish. Whisk together the garlic, ginger, chilli, lime juice and fish sauce and pour it over the chicken. Stir to coat, then cover in clingfilm and marinate in the fridge for at least 1 hour.

Preheat the grill to high. Thread a strip of chicken on to each skewer (as shown right) and cook for about 3 minutes on each side, until the chicken is browned and cooked through.

To make the sauce, put the coconut milk, peanut butter, garlic, chilli and juice from ½ a lime in a bowl and whisk to combine using a fork. Season with soy sauce and more lime juice to taste, then spoon into a small serving bowl. Serve with the chicken satay, for dipping.

tropical fruit skewers
Makes 12

Juicy tropical fruits threaded on skewers make a pretty and refreshing palate cleanser between the savouries and cakes on this menu. You can vary the choice of fruits if you like: papaya or kiwi and star fruit are all good.

3 small ripe mangoes
½ lime
3 bananas
350 g lychees, peeled and pitted
fresh mint leaves, to garnish
12 wooden or bamboo skewers

Using a sharp knife, slice the flesh away from each side of the mango stone. Cut each slice in half, then slice the flesh away from the skin and discard the skin. Cut each piece of flesh into three small wedges. Squeeze a little lime juice over each piece.

Peel the bananas and cut them into slices 1.5 cm thick. Thread pieces of fruit on the skewers and arrange on a serving platter. Garnish with the mint leaves and serve.

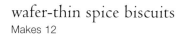

wafer-thin spice biscuits
Makes 12

Inspired by the flavours of the Indonesian spice islands, these giant, wafer-thin biscuits are the perfect accompaniment to the fresh fruit skewers. They're so light and crisp that you can just imagine biting into one as you sit on a shady verandah and enjoy the cooling sea breeze.

25 g plain flour
¼ teaspoon ground cinnamon
¼ teaspoon freshly grated nutmeg
50 g soft brown sugar
1 egg white
25 g butter, melted
2 baking trays, greased
a rolling pin, for shaping biscuits

Preheat the oven to 190°C (375°F) Gas 5.

Sift the flour, cinnamon and nutmeg into a bowl and set aside. Break up the brown sugar with a fork, fluffing it up to make sure that there are no lumps, then set aside.

Put the egg white in a separate, grease-free bowl and whisk to form peaks. Sprinkle in about one-third of the sugar and whisk in, then whisk in the remaining two-thirds in the same way. Sift in the flour mixture and drizzle in the butter, then fold together to make a thick, creamy batter.

Working with one baking tray at a time, drop a small tablespoonful of the batter on to the tray and spread it out to make an 8-cm round. Repeat to

make one or two more biscuits, depending on the size of your baking tray. Bake for about 5 minutes, until the biscuits are browning round the edges.

Remove the baking tray from the oven and immediately slide a spatula under the biscuits, lift them from the tray and drape over a rolling pin to cool. They will take on a curved shape as they crisp up.

Continue in the same way until all the batter has been used up. (You can prepare one tray of biscuit mixture while the other bakes.)

pineapple cake with lime syrup
Serves 8–12

This moist cake, made with soft brown sugar and drenched with a sweet yet tangy lime syrup, provides a stunning centrepiece for a tropically themed tea. Serve it plain or with a dollop of whipped cream on the side.

140 g butter, at room temperature
150 g light brown sugar
3 eggs
175 g self-raising flour
½ teaspoon ground ginger
4 tablespoons crème fraîche
227-g can pineapple rings, drained and diced
a 20-cm diameter cake tin, lined with greaseproof paper

FOR THE LIME SYRUP
finely grated zest and freshly squeezed juice of 2 unwaxed limes
85 g caster sugar

Preheat the oven to 180°C (350°F) Gas 4. Put the butter and sugar in a bowl and beat until smooth and fluffy. Beat in the eggs one at a time. Sift in the flour

and ginger and stir in, then fold in the crème fraîche followed by the pineapple. Spoon the mixture into the prepared cake tin and level the surface. Bake for about 50 minutes, until risen and golden and a skewer inserted in the centre of the cake comes out clean. Turn out on to a wire rack to cool.

To make the syrup, put the lime zest in a saucepan. Add the lime juice and sugar. Heat gently, stirring constantly, until the sugar has dissolved, then bring to the boil. Boil for about 1 minute only, then remove from the heat. Leave the syrup to cool until it thickens slightly, then pour it over the cake. Let stand for about 30 minutes before serving.

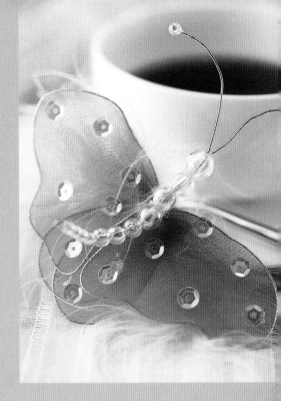

Sweet Sixteen

fruity vanilla 'tea'

peanut butter and
jam sandwiches

love heart sugar cookies

sparkly tiara cupcakes

Any sixteenth birthday celebration should be a fabulously girly affair and this gorgeous themed party will not disappoint. Don't hold back on the décor and dress the room with twinkling fairy lights, feather boas and just about anything that takes your fancy – as long as it's pink! The food is delightfully, deliciously pretty and the recipes very simple to follow, so the food can either be prepared ahead of time or made an integral part of the afternoon – the birthday girl and her guests can enjoy a girly gossip and a giggle as they bake and decorate the cookies and cupcakes.

fruity vanilla 'tea'
Serves 4

Light, fruity infusions are the ideal vehicle for fragrant vanilla and this lovely tea has just the right blend of sweetness and sophistication for this menu.

1 vanilla pod
4 red berry fruit 'tea' bags
   of your choice
clear honey, to taste

Pour some boiling water into a large teapot and leave it to warm. Meanwhile, fill the kettle with water and set it to boil.

Split the vanilla pod in half lengthways. When the kettle is coming to the boil, drain the teapot and add the vanilla pod and tea bags. Pour in boiling water and leave to infuse for about 5 minutes, then pour into cups through a strainer to catch any vanilla seeds. Sweeten to taste with honey.

FRUIT INFUSIONS
A caffeine-free drink is what's needed for this young persons' tea party, so a fruity infusion is the perfect choice. Look out for red berry 'teas' such as raspberry, strawberry or a blend of summer berries with a hint of vanilla. Whatever you choose, make it in a large teapot and serve with a little dish of clear honey to sweeten.

peanut butter and jam sandwiches

Makes 12

These cute-as-a-button little sandwiches, with strawberry jam hearts, are the ultimate in girly kitsch.

6 slices soft white bread
8 tablespoons smooth peanut butter
4 tablespoons strawberry jam
*a heart-shaped biscuit cutter,
2.5 cm diameter*

Lay three slices of bread on a board and score them lightly from corner to corner into quarters. Stamp out a heart shape from the centre of each quarter. Set aside.

Spread the remaining three slices of bread with peanut butter, then spread a thinner layer of strawberry jam over the top. Place the slices of bread with hearts stamped out of them on top and pat down gently.

Gently lay your hand on top of the sandwich and using a serrated knife and a gentle sawing motion, cut off the crusts. Cut the sandwiches crossways into quarters between the hearts. Arrange on a plate to serve.

love heart sugar cookies

Makes about 20

These delicate, buttery sugar cookies are fun to make and look very pretty piled up on a plate on the tea table.

115 g butter, at room temperature
50 g caster sugar
1 egg yolk
175 g plain flour
*2 baking trays, greased
a heart-shaped biscuit cutter,
6.5 cm diameter*

TO DECORATE
1 tablespoon granulated sugar
red food colouring
75 g white chocolate

Put the butter and sugar in a bowl and beat until pale and creamy. Beat in the egg yolk. Stir in the flour, then knead the mixture gently to make a soft dough. Wrap in clingfilm and chill for about 30 minutes.

Preheat the oven to 180°C (350°F) Gas 4. Gently roll out the dough on a lightly floured surface to a thickness of about 4 mm. Stamp out shapes using a biscuit cutter and arrange them on the baking trays. Re-roll the trimmings to cut out more cookies.

Bake for about 10 minutes, until a pale golden colour. Leave the cookies on the baking trays to cool for a few minutes then transfer to a wire rack to cool.

To decorate, put the sugar in a bowl and add a few drops of food colouring. Work the colouring into the sugar until evenly coloured and pink. Melt the chocolate in a heatproof bowl set over a pan of gently simmering water. Drizzle lines of chocolate around the outside edge of each cookie. Sprinkle with pink sugar and leave to set.

sparkly tiara cupcakes
Makes 12

These are the ultimate cupcakes
for princesses everywhere!

115 g butter, at room temperature
115 g caster sugar
2 eggs
115 g self-raising flour
1 teaspoon vanilla extract
2 tablespoons full-fat milk
a 12-hole cupcake tin, lined with plain
  or patterned paper cases

TO DECORATE
185 g icing sugar, sifted
1 egg white
lilac food colouring
about 6 clear red boiled sweets
edible sparkles and edible silver balls

Preheat the oven to 180°C (350°F)
Gas 4. Put the butter and sugar in a
large bowl and beat until pale and fluffy.
Beat in the eggs, one at a time. Sift
over the flour and fold in, then fold in
the vanilla extract and milk. Spoon the
mixture into the paper cases, then
bake for about 17 minutes, until risen
and golden and a skewer inserted in
the centre of a cake comes out clean.
Transfer to a wire rack and let cool
completely before decorating.

To decorate, leave the sweets in their
wrappers and tap with a rolling pin to
break into large pieces. Set aside. To
make the icing, gradually beat the icing
sugar into the egg white until smooth and
creamy, then beat in a few drops of food
colouring until the desired colour has
been achieved. Spread the icing on top
of the cakes. Pile a little heap of boiled
sweet 'jewels' in the centre of each cake
and sprinkle with edible sparkles and
silver balls. Let set slightly before serving.

Big Top Tea

fruity tea punch

'strongman' tuna, sweetcorn
and spinach sandwiches

the big dipper

clown cookies

big top cake

Tea parties are great fun for children and this circus-themed party

is perfect for a birthday celebration. If you want to go down the

fancy-dress route, invite the children to come dressed as circus

characters such as a clown, ringmaster, lion tamer or strongman.

Go to your local party shop and see if they have some circus-themed

paper plates, cups and napkins. Buy some brightly-coloured helium-

filled balloons to tie to each child's chair, to create a magical fantasy

world in which the children can enjoy their special tea party.

fruity tea punch
Makes 8 small glasses

2 fruit tea bags of your choice
2½ tablespoons caster sugar
600 ml fresh orange juice
225 g strawberries, washed, hulled
   and thinly sliced

Put the tea bags in a heatproof
jug or bowl and pour over about
600 ml boiling water. Leave
to infuse for 5 minutes, then
remove the tea bags and stir
in the sugar. Leave to cool.

When cool, stir in the orange
juice and chill until ready
to serve. To serve, add the
strawberry slices and pour
or ladle into cups or glasses.

FRUITY PUNCH

A caffeine-free fruit infusion makes a great party punch for
a children's tea party. Serve it in a large punch bowl with a
ladle and scoop it into party cups, making sure each child
gets plenty of fresh strawberries.

'strongman' tuna, sweetcorn and spinach sandwiches

Makes 12

These little tuna sandwiches are packed with healthy fresh spinach and guaranteed to build extra-big muscles on little strongmen (and women)!

185-g tin tuna in brine or oil, well drained
2–3 tablespoons mayonnaise
4 tablespoons tinned sweetcorn kernels (optional)
butter, for spreading, at room temperature
6 slices wholegrain bread
a handful of baby spinach leaves
freshly ground black pepper

Put the tuna in a bowl and break it up into flakes using a fork. Add the mayonnaise and mix to combine. Add the sweetcorn, if using, and season to taste with a little pepper.

Butter the slices of bread, then divide the tuna and sweetcorn mixture between three of the slices and spread it evenly over the top. Top each slice with baby spinach leaves and follow with a second slice of bread. Press down gently.

Using a serrated knife, gently slice off the crusts and cut each sandwich into four small triangles. Cover with clingfilm until ready to serve, to stop the bread from drying out and curling up.

the big dipper

Serves 6–8

Kids love dips and this sweet yet tangy one makes a healthy treat.

½ butternut squash, deseeded, peeled and cut into chunks
2 red peppers, cored and chopped
1 tablespoon olive oil
½ garlic clove
1 teaspoon cider vinegar
6 fresh basil leaves, finely chopped
sea salt and freshly ground black pepper
plain tortilla chips, cucumber batons and celery sticks, to serve

Preheat the oven to 190°C (375°F) Gas 5. Put the squash and red pepper in a baking dish, drizzle with ½ tablespoon of oil, season and toss to coat. Roast for about 35 minutes, tossing once or twice, until tender. Set aside to cool.

Put the roasted vegetables in a blender and add the garlic and vinegar. Blend until smooth. Stir in the basil and season to taste. Use a spatula to scrape the dip into a serving bowl. Serve with tortilla chips, cucumber batons and celery sticks for dipping.

clown cookies

Makes 12

Funny-faced clowns are always the highlight of any circus. With their big red noses and curly-wurly hair, no one will be able to resist these fun cookies. They may look complicated but are very easy to decorate and children will adore them.

100 g butter, at room temperature
50 g icing sugar
grated zest of ½ unwaxed orange
1 egg yolk
150 g plain flour
a biscuit cutter, 7.5 cm diameter

TO DECORATE
25 g butter, at room temperature
75 g icing sugar, sifted
1 teaspoon milk
5 glacé cherries, halved
fruit strings in assorted colours,
   or red and black liquorice laces
red and black icing writers

Put the butter and sugar in a bowl and beat together until smooth and creamy. Beat in the orange zest and egg yolk. Add the flour and mix to make a smooth, soft dough. Wrap in clingfilm and chill for at least 1 hour.

Preheat the oven to 200°C (400°F) Gas 6. Roll out the cookie dough on a lightly floured surface and stamp out rounds using a biscuit cutter. Re-roll the trimmings to make more rounds. Place the rounds on a greased baking tray.

Bake for 10–12 minutes, until a pale golden colour around the edges. Leave to cool on the baking tray for about 2 minutes, then transfer to a wire rack to cool.

To decorate, beat together the butter, icing sugar and milk until creamy, then use a blob to attach a glacé cherry 'nose' to the centre of each cookie. Spread a little more buttercream along the top edge of each cookie, then twist a strand of fruit string on top to make curly hair, pressing it gently to fix it in place.

Using black icing writers, make two crosses for eyes, then use a red one to draw a mouth. Let the icing set before serving.

big top cake
Serves 8–12

This cake is incredibly simple to make and decorate, yet creates a stunning centrepiece for a circus-themed tea party. To make it even more special, search out animal-shaped biscuits such as tigers, lions or circus ponies and prop these up around the cake.

180 g butter, at room temperature
180 g caster sugar
3 eggs
180 g self-raising flour
1½ teaspoons vanilla extract

TO DECORATE
60 g butter, at room temperature
140 g icing sugar, sifted
1 tablespoon full-fat milk
a few drops of vanilla extract
5 tablespoons strawberry jam
about 450 g ready-rolled white
    fondant icing
red food colouring
9 cm x 3 cm piece of coloured card
a cocktail stick
2 x 20-cm diameter sandwich tins,
    greased and lined

Preheat the oven to 180°C (350°F) Gas 4.

Put the butter and sugar in a bowl and beat until pale and fluffy. Beat in the eggs one at a time. Sift in the flour and mix to thoroughly combine. Stir in the vanilla extract.

Spoon the cake mixture into the prepared tins and level the surface of each. Bake for 20–25 minutes, until golden brown and the sponge springs back when pressed lightly with the tips of your fingers. Turn the cakes out on to a wire rack, gently peel off the lining paper and leave to cool completely.

To decorate, beat the butter until soft, then add the icing sugar, milk and vanilla extract, and beat until smooth and creamy. Spread a layer of buttercream over the cake, then spread with 3 tablespoons of the jam. Place the second cake on top and press down very gently.

Trim the fondant icing to a round of about 30 cm in diameter. Force the remaining 2 tablespoons of jam through a sieve (to remove the pips) and put it in a small saucepan. Add ½ teaspoon water, then warm gently, stirring. Brush the melted jam over the cake, then gently lay the fondant icing on top, smoothing it down over the top and sides of the cake. Trim off any excess with a sharp knife.

Using a clean paintbrush and the red food colouring, paint red stripes on the fondant icing, starting at the centre, to resemble the stripes on a circus 'big top' tent.

Fold the piece of card in half and place the cocktail stick in the fold to make a flag, then use sticky tape to secure it in place. Cut a triangle out of the end of the flag to give pointed ends, then stick the flag in the centre of the cake to finish.

Teddy Bear's Picnic

lemon tea punch

baby picnic quiches

gingerbread teddy bears

honey buns

grizzly bear bars

This tea party theme could not be any cuter. You can enjoy an adorable retro children's tea party indoors or out. Create a faux picnic setting indoors by laying out chequered picnic rugs on the floor and setting out picnic hampers full of plates and cups. Invite the children to bring their favourite teddy to sit with them at the party. Alternatively, take the picnic outdoors – either into the garden or to the park or other local beauty spot. Simply pack up the food in a hamper or coolbox, pour the punch into a thermos flask, and set off for some good old-fashioned fun in the fresh air!

baby picnic quiches
Makes 12

Little quiches speckled with sweet onion and bacon are great for picnics. They're perfect to pack in a hamper, and small hands can pick them up easily – children won't be able to resist.

FOR THE PASTRY
85 g plain flour
40 g chilled butter, diced
1 tablespoon iced water
a biscuit cutter, 6.5 cm diameter
a 12-hole mini tartlet tin

FOR THE FILLING
1 tablespoon olive oil
¼ small onion
1 rasher lean bacon, snipped into
    small pieces
2 tablespoons mascarpone cheese
2 tablespoons double cream
1 egg
snipped chives, for sprinkling
sea salt and freshly ground
    black pepper

To make the pastry, put the flour, a pinch of salt and diced butter in a food processor and process until the mixture resembles fine breadcrumbs. Gradually add 1 tablespoon iced water until the mixture comes together. Press into a ball, wrap in clingfilm and chill for 30 minutes.

Preheat the oven to 190°C (375°F) Gas 5. Meanwhile, heat the olive oil in a non-stick frying pan and fry the onion for about 3 minutes. Add the bacon and fry for a further 3 minutes until cooked and the onion is soft.

LEMON TEA PUNCH
This refreshing drink is somewhere between a lemon squash, an old-fashioned lemonade and iced lemon tea and is great for children. Decant it into a thermos for a picnic, or pour into a large ice-filled jug to serve at the table.

lemon tea punch
Makes 1.2 litres

1 large lemon, thinly sliced
4 tablespoons caster sugar
1.2 litres boiling water

Put the lemon and any juice in a large bowl and sprinkle the sugar on top. Pour in boiling water and leave to infuse for about 5 minutes, then strain. Leave to cool, then chill until ready to serve.

Combine the mascarpone and cream, then stir in the bacon and onion. Add the egg, a pinch of salt and a grinding of pepper and mix to combine. Set aside.

Roll out the pastry on a lightly floured surface and cut out in to rounds using a biscuit cutter. Press the rounds into the tartlet tin and prick the bases with a fork. Bake for about 5 minutes, then remove from the oven and spoon about a tablespoonful of filling into each tart. Sprinkle chives over each one and return them to the oven to bake for a further 15 minutes, until golden and the filling is risen and set.

Remove from the oven and transfer to a wire rack to cool.

gingerbread teddy bears
Makes about 10

Look out for teddy-bear-shaped biscuit cutters in kitchen shops. Ready-made coloured icing sold in squeezy tubes make it easier for small children to help with the decorating.

115 g butter
2 tablespoons golden syrup
350 g plain flour
1 teaspoon bicarbonate of soda
1 teaspoon ground ginger
175 g soft brown sugar
1 egg, beaten
teddy bear-shaped biscuit cutters in assorted sizes
2 baking trays, greased
icing tubes in assorted colours and edible balls, to decorate

Warm the butter and syrup in a saucepan until melted, then set aside to cool. Combine the flour, bicarbonate of soda, ginger and sugar in a bowl. Make a well in the centre. Pour in the butter and syrup, add the egg, then mix well to combine. Knead lightly to form a soft dough, then wrap it in clingfilm and chill for about 20 minutes. Preheat the oven to 190°C

(375°F) Gas 5. Roll out the dough on a lightly floured surface and stamp out shapes using biscuit cutters. Transfer the shapes to the baking trays and bake for 7–8 minutes, until starting to colour around the edges. Leave to cool on the trays for about 3 minutes, then transfer to a wire rack to cool completely. Decorate the bears as desired.

honey buns
Makes 12

Bears love honey, so they'll love these sticky little honey buns too. Older children will enjoy helping to decorate the cakes in preparation for their teddy bear's picnic, so why not let them help with spooning on the icing and adding the sprinkles.

60 g butter
50 g caster sugar
4 tablespoons clear honey
80 ml full-fat milk
1 egg, beaten
115 g self-raising flour
a 12-hole cupcake tin, lined with paper cases

TO DECORATE
200 g icing sugar, sifted
2 tablespoons freshly squeezed lemon juice
assorted coloured sprinkles

Preheat the oven to 170°C (325°F) Gas 3.

Put the butter, sugar and honey in a saucepan and warm gently, stirring constantly, until the butter has melted. Remove the pan from the heat and stir in the milk. Stir in the egg, then sift in the flour and stir in.

Spoon the mixture into the paper cases and bake for about 20 minutes, until golden and risen. Leave the cakes to cool in the tin for a couple of minutes, then transfer to a wire rack to cool completely.

To decorate, stir the lemon juice into the icing sugar until you have a thick, spoonable consistency. If necessary, add a little more lemon juice. Spoon the icing on to the cakes and finish with coloured sprinkles. Let set before serving.

grizzly bear bars
Makes 14

You'll need big grizzly bear teeth to chew on these delicious nutty and fudgy bars. They're quite rich and sweet so you might want to cut them into smaller squares for very young children.

175 g plain flour
115 g chilled butter, diced
50 g caster sugar
a 20-cm square cake tin, greased and lined

FOR THE TOPPING
50 g butter
50 g light muscovado sugar
397-g tin sweetened condensed milk
40 g hazelnuts
50 g brazil nuts, halved
25 g pistachio nuts
40 g plain chocolate, melted

Preheat the oven to 180°C (350°F) Gas 4. Put the flour in a bowl, add the butter and toss to coat in flour, then rub in until the mixture resembles breadcrumbs. Add the sugar and stir in, then bring together into a pliable dough. Press the dough into the prepared tin to cover the base, using the back of a spoon to press down and smooth out the surface. Prick the surface all over with a fork and bake for about 25 minutes, until light brown and firm to the touch. Set aside to cool.

While the shortbread is still slightly warm, put the butter, sugar and condensed milk in a saucepan and heat gently, stirring constantly, until the sugar dissolves. Bring to the boil, then simmer gently over low heat for about 10 minutes, stirring constantly. Remove from the heat, stir in the nuts, then pour the caramel mixture over the shortbread base. Spread out in an even layer and leave to cool. Drizzle with melted chocolate and let set. Use a knife to slice the shortbread in to bars or squares.

Useful Websites

BAKING EQUIPMENT

CAKES, COOKIES & CRAFTS SHOP
www.cakescookiesandcrafts
shop.co.uk
Tel: 01524 389 684
*Online suppliers of every kind
of baking equipment including
paper cupcake cases, cake
and muffin tins, biscuit cutters
and edible decorations.*

LAKELAND
www.lakeland.co.uk
Tel: 01539 488 100
*A huge selection of kitchen
and baking equipment, such as
cupcake tins, cake decorations
and storage containers.*

JANE ASHER
www.janeasher.com
22–24 Cale Street
London SW3 3QU
Tel: 020 7584 6177
*Britain's foremost cake and
sugarcraft supplier, for all
your decorating needs!*

DAVID MELLOR
www.davidmellordesign.com
4 Sloane Square
London SW1W 8EE
Tel: 020 7730 4259
*Well-stocked kitchen shop
and online store.*

JOHN LEWIS
www.johnlewis.com
*A range of bakeware, from
vintage-style mixing bowls
and measuring cups to
silicone cupcake tins.*

DIVERTIMENTI
www.divertimenti.co.uk
227–229 Brompton Road
London SW3 2EP
Tel: 020 7581 8065
33–34 Marylebone High Street
London W1U 4PT
Tel: 020 7935 0689
*Divertimenti shops in South
Kensington and the West End
stock an enormous range of
hand-decorated tableware,
cutlery and glassware.
Their online shop is equally
comprehensive, with individual,
reusable silicone muffin and
cupcake cases.*

CHINA AND TABLE LINENS

CHINASEARCH
www.chinasearch.co.uk
Tel: 01926 512402
*Europe's largest china-matching
service, supplying discontinued
replacement tableware and
china worldwide, including a
wonderful selection of vintage
cake stands.*

EMMA BRIDGEWATER
www.emmabridgewater.co.uk
Tel: 020 7371 5489
*Finest-quality ceramic kitchen
and tableware, including a
wide range of teapots, cups
and mugs with distinctive,
colourful patterns. Cake tins
and biscuit barrels are also
available plus kitchen linens.
Buy online or from shops
nationwide. See website for
details of stockists.*

CATH KIDSTON
www.cathkidston.co.uk
Tel: 0845 026 2440
*Retro-inspired homewares
including beautiful tablecloths,
napkins and china in trademark
floral, spotted and striped
prints. Buy online or from
shops nationwide. See website
for details of stockists.*

THOMAS GOODE & CO
www.thomasgoode.co.uk
19 South Audley Street
Mayfair
London W1K 2BN
Tel: 020 7499 2823
*Considered by some to be the
best fine bone china, crystal
and silverware shop in the
world, this is the destination
for dressing the ultimate
afternoon tea party table!*

GRAHAM & GREEN
www.grahamandgreen.co.uk
Tel: 0845 130 6622
*Online boutique selling beautiful
accessories, gifts and interior
items, including tea sets, cake
stands, large jugs (suitable for
iced teas and punches), and
Moroccan tea glasses.*

PLUMO
www.plumo.com
Tel: 0870 241 3590
*An online boutique selling lovely
home accessories including
tea sets, silver-plated tea
caddies and a selection of
tiered, vintage-style glass
cake stands.*

SOMETHING
www.something-shop.com
58 Lamb's Conduit Street
Bloomsbury
London WC1N 3LW
Tel: 020 7430 1516
Gorgeous gift shop selling beautiful glass cake stands and vintage tea plates.

TEA MERCHANTS

CLIPPER TEAS
www.clipper-teas.com
An award-winning range of organic, fairtrade teas and infusions including traditional blends and new classics, all available to buy online.

FORTNUM AND MASON
www.fortnumandmason.com
181 Piccadilly
London W1A 1ER
Tel: 020 7734 8040
Famed for its sumptuous food hall, this famous London shop sells many fine teas, including its own exclusive blends, plus tea-making accoutrements, all available to buy online.

WHITTARD OF CHELSEA
www.whittard.co.uk
38 Covent Garden Market
London WC2E 8RF
Tel: 020 7379 6599
In addition to fine teas and coffees, Whittard's shops nationwide sell an array of colourful, ever-changing seasonal ceramics. See website for details.

Conversion Charts

Weights and measures have been rounded up or down slightly to make measuring easier.

Measuring butter:
A US stick of butter weighs 4 oz. which is approximately 115 g or 8 tablespoons.

The recipes in this book require the following conversions:

American	Metric	Imperial
6 tbsp	85 g	3 oz.
7 tbsp	100 g	3½ oz.
1 stick	115 g	4 oz.

Volume equivalents:

American	Metric	Imperial
1 teaspoon	5 ml	
1 tablespoon	15 ml	
¼ cup	60 ml	2 fl. oz.
⅓ cup	75 ml	2½ fl. oz.
½ cup	125 ml	4 fl. oz.
⅔ cup	150 ml	5 fl. oz. (¼ pint)
¾ cup	175 ml	6 fl. oz.
1 cup	250 ml	8 fl. oz.

Weight equivalents:		Measurements:	
Imperial	Metric	Inches	cm
1 oz.	30 g	¼ inch	5 mm
2 oz.	55 g	½ inch	1 cm
3 oz.	85 g	1 inch	2.5 cm
3½ oz.	100 g	2 inches	5 cm
4 oz.	115 g	3 inches	7 cm
6 oz.	175 g	4 inches	10 cm
8 oz. (½ lb.)	225 g	5 inches	12 cm
9 oz.	250 g	6 inches	15 cm
10 oz.	280 g	7 inches	18 cm
12 oz.	350 g	8 inches	20 cm
13 oz.	375 g	9 inches	23 cm
14 oz.	400 g	10 inches	25 cm
15 oz.	425 g	11 inches	28 cm
16 oz. (1 lb.)	450 g	12 inches	30 cm

Oven temperatures:

120°C	(250°F)	Gas ½
140°C	(275°F)	Gas 1
150°C	(300°F)	Gas 2
170°C	(325°F)	Gas 3
180°C	(350°F)	Gas 4
190°C	(375°F)	Gas 5
200°C	(400°F)	Gas 6
220°C	(425°F)	Gas 7

Index

Credits

The publisher would like to thank Farley Prop Hire for use of locations for the following stories:

Bridal Shower (page 66-73), French-style Tea (page 52–57), Southern-style Tea (page 74–79) and Big Top Tea (page 128–133).

Contact them on 020 8749 9925 or visit www.farley.co.uk for further information

Image for endpapers taken from Weaving Patterns published by The Pepin Press www.pepinpress.com